The Sacred Secrets of Vesta

The Sacred Secrets of Vesta

The Astrology of Kundalini Rising

Rachel McCabe

Ellhorn Press
Hubbardston, Massachusetts

Ellhorn Press
12 Simonds Hill Road
Hubbardston, MA 01452

The Sacred Secrets of Vesta: The Astrology of Kundalini Rising
© 2022 Rachel McCabe
ISBN 978-1-7345032-2-7

All rights reserved.
No part of this book may be reproduced in any form
or by any means without the permission of the author.

Printed in cooperation with
Lulu Enterprises, Inc.
860 Aviation Parkway, Suite 300
Morrisville, NC 27560

*I want to give thanks to all my teachers,
those before me and all who come after.
Thank you!*

Contents

Part 1: History and Holiness
The Beginnings of Vesta 1
The Greek Goddess Hestia 10
The Myths and Origins of Vesta 14
The Vestals in History and the Present 26
Vesta and the Other Goddesses 43

Part 2: In the Stars
Vesta in Astrology 65
Vesta in the Signs 70
Vesta in the Houses/Temples 77
The Vesta Forum: Aspects 85

Part 3: Mystery and Mirroring
More Secrets of Vesta 125
Psychology/Biology and Vesta 130
Sacred Rites and Relics of Vesta 137
Modern Vestal Women and Sexuality 151
Kundalini Rising 165
Epilogue: The Will of Vesta 185

References 186

Introduction

This book was extremely challenging to finish. The goal of Vesta is not for the accolades; her goal is spiritual growth. Trying to complete a book like this is like trying to end a life and willfully entering death. Thus came the acceptance of death as just another transition of life.

Sharing with others is paramount, but it is not the uplifting of self; it is the uplifting of all. That is the goal. I am human and possess an ego, but this isn't about me. I do want to share my experiences and activations. But how does one speak about the unspeakable? That is, our experiences that are only communicable or conveyable to those who have experienced similar occurrences. One cannot be an expert in the things never experienced, but I learned ample amounts about Vesta through my guru. However, I did not realize this when it was happening. I have become aware of Vesta through my recent transitions. We are, perhaps, initiates of Vesta (Vesta prominent in the birth chart or an initiate of the god/goddess herself). I will often refer to people with Vesta prominent in the birth chart as **Vestals** in this book. But anyone can connect to the goddess of the threshold.

The Sacred Secrets of Vesta came into being from a journey that I recorded in my Tantra diary. I became interested in Tantra when orgasm had become difficult. I was already a naturalist, and I became naturally magnetized by the root of this ancient wisdom. A guru appeared—someone familiar and respected. Through my journal, I documented my honest, soul-shaking experiences. After I experienced a kundalini-rising, my interest in Tantra grew. It was a highly erotic and personal account, some of whose entries I have included in this book.

I came to Vesta when I began to focus on high spiritual matters. Soul-raising, love of the moment, connection with life, the cosmos; the living, breathing energy of the highest self! By practicing Tantra rituals by myself, encouraged by my guru, I learned how to trust again. It helped me to work through trauma and to love everything, even the not-so-savory things, about myself. Things continue to come to the surface to work through. There is a higher power and all one has to do is desire to connect with it.

I had to become the embodiment of the virgin goddess to write this book. My experience with Shakti energy inspired me, the spark of the virgin fire set ablaze. And then it became constricted and self-contained. When I decided to put this goddess to work, I thought my marriage was fine, but I was experiencing a lack. Change occurred to provide that desire. Suddenly the idea that everything was fine was ripped away. Something happened, to my dismay, and tore apart my family. I had no control over the situation. I "left it to God", so to speak. Vesta was already waiting when I asked for help.

The desire materialized, but I was not able to surrender to it. We often desire things that may not be good for us or others, but nevertheless the desire is there. My vows to Vesta limit me from expressing that desire. I later had to go back to when I first felt or made the desire known, and changed it for a safer, healthier expression.

I have compared a Vestal to "the sacred slut with a chastity belt from god/goddess". That is how I felt. Sex is not everything, and desires can be transmuted into higher desire, and therefore, a higher vibration. Vesta works with desires. She is not necessarily involved in creating the desire, but she presents the opportunity to overcome or transmute desire. She often denies her own desires for the sake of others, and therefore she is linked to renunciation. It takes an incredible amount of strength to balance passion and desire. Faithfulness is tested.

According to the wisdom and teachings of Kabbalah, we have two desires: the desire to receive for the self alone, and the desire to receive the light in order to share it with others. Vesta transmutes desire for self into the desire to serve. She is present during times of transition: guardian of the threshold to transformation, adoption/change of family, marriage/divorce, sex changes/major life adjustments, adolescence, middle age, retirement, death, and other initiations.

Through my deep experiences (Vesta conjunct Pluto ... I often associate Vesta with sexual energy, but Vesta can manifest as other energies as well) and the information I have studied on Vesta, other goddesses, and planets I have formed the foundation of this work. It is the result of my astrological and spiritual studies thus far. Constant work and pressure is required to keep going.

Vesta is linked to Virgo. She is a hard-working, service-oriented hermit. She loves her home environment and her sacred space. Late nights and peaceful retreats allow her to be at her best. Also, Vesta needs Saturn and his discipline. Chiron was also a player for me in 2020/2021(my husband's Chiron return); Chiron is the healer of wounds, after all. Separated from my husband/family, I wanted to die. Then I wanted to join a monastery. Then I wanted to be bound and whipped. I felt the need to be disciplined. Chiron taught me discipline when Saturn was unavailable.

I was experiencing yet another transition. I later learned that this process is essential to the priest(ess) entering the position of a Vestal (renunciate). You leave your old life and family for a new one. Relying on the Church or temple (higher authority), you essentially die and are reborn, married to that higher authority; God/Goddess, Sofia or Christ. You enter into a new life, typically in a monastery or isolation.

Most monasteries today incorporate the ancient Vestal way of being: a ceremony or marriage takes place, vows are given, and disciplines are submitted to. Some nuns flog themselves with leather straps as a way to endure the sufferings of Christ. Pain infliction is a discipline. If you are punished for making a mistake, then you would not make the mistake again. Flagellation, pain, and sacrifice are common practices among many spiritual cultures.

Vesta is currently transiting Scorpio and my 12th house. I have Vesta prominent in my chart, and I have had a hard time deciding where to devote my focus. When I made the vow of celibacy, I did not think about how long I would be celibate for. I hope it's not 30 years, even though that is how long a Roman Vestal had to be devoted.

From my journal:

There are so many different paths. I can spin in circles for a long time. My energy rises and falls. I don't eat. I can't sleep. I want to love and be loved, but at this time it is all misdirected. Swimming around like fish caught in an undertow. I feel excited about the future and terrified about living in the past. My kundalini energy is strong. It is how to focus my energy. If I can flow and bring the attention to the now; the goal in mind. Set to work and breathe. So much work. One day at a time until the 30-year cycle is complete. Then a new focus will arrive.

A Vestal virgin was to serve for 30 years, which is the number of degrees in one sign. In astrological progressions, every 30 years the Sun sign and Ascendant changes or has changed; about one degree a year.

From my journal:

My husband did something that I forgave immediately; however, I was not able to get the thought out of my head. Sex had become painful. I no longer desired that part of him. I still love him, but I feel we have been severed. In that moment the goddess requested I make vows to her. I did in an instant. I felt I had no other choice.

My devotion belongs to the Goddess. I have become closed off to others entering my temple. I have made vows to the goddess of chastity and eroticism. Although, I feel more sexual; even celibates masturbate. My smell has changed and I love it. I feel like the bud of a cannabis plant. My pollen, crystals, and sweet nectar have become more potent, abundant, and succulent with the absence of the male stamen. In the female plant, her euphoria expands as her physical searches in almost desperation for her male counterpart. This can be a powerful experience to awaken her masculine force. Some plants will even transform into hermaphrodites for procreation. They have become their own creative force.

Saturn, father of Vesta, is seen in Capricorn. I read that Saturn transits can represent a time of celibacy, and perhaps limitations and sacrifice. I know many Capricorns and, as an Earth sign, they can have a very sexual nature. When I took vows of celibacy I noticed that my progressed ascendant is moving into Capricorn, and I also noticed the current (2020), Capricorn stellium (a group of three or more planets conjunct or close together).

A Vestal, or Vesta prominent is someone who has the Sun, Moon, or a stellium of planets in aspect with Vesta. Other prominent points, such as the Ascendant, are also good indicators. Vesta relates to Virgo, the virgin, and Scorpio, the transformer. When I refer to "her" in this book, know that I am also referring to "him". Although Vesta and Vestal Virgins are considered feminine, men are just as likely to have a strong Vesta in their natal charts. A strong Vesta is often surrounded by the opposite sex, or the same-sex pertaining to the youthful feminine.

My journey into Vesta, both the goddess and the planetoid, has come at a time after spiritual isolation when I am attracting some attention. I seem to need to teach others about these sacred rites. They are so healing, but it brings some emotional baggage. It is the Vestals' job to soak up all the negative or sexually aggressive energy and transmute it through alchemy. The problem, however, is that often the sexual aggressive energy wants an outlet and some seek to fulfill it in a not-so-loving way. Vesta has the ability to put a stop to that; Vesta brings the love and burns everything else. If she is treated with love and devotion she grants the player liberation. By worshiping the goddess/woman/self in this manner one gains power over his life.

I want to be of service; I realized that when going through my ordeal. The hardest part of teaching, especially about sacred sexuality, is the emotional, physical, and mental evolvement. People bring all of their beings into sacred sexuality. Tantra, though, is not all about sex. It is about the joy of living wholly in the present.

Later from my journal:

Part of Vesta is kinky sexual desire. Embodying her, I must experience all of her. My secret sexual desire is rising to the surface. Although I have made vows of chastity to the goddess herself, she is revealing to me my sexual nature. I can express this without breaking my vows. However, it is so dark and involves another to partake; it is, therefore, potentially dangerous.

...Unobstructed wantonness. She is the tantrika that accepts her sexuality in its full expression. That means being able to express one's whole self, devoid of shame, guilt, and disgust. This is going to take time and work to get through these blocks as the world often perceives a woman in her full sexuality as negative. A woman who has sex out of wedlock or with whomever she chooses is often considered unclean or licentious.

Vesta has been associated with the sacred slut. In some cultures, including ancient India, there were priestesses who provided sacred service. In many ancient cultures (and reflected in astrology) every part or aspect of the human anatomy is sacred. The "slut" is usually depicted as a "dirty woman" of a lower class, a servant that does the housework. Not usually associated with men (even promiscuous ones), it also means "a person who lacks the ability or chooses not to exercise a power of discernment to order her affairs".

Identification with the image of an erotic woman brings up all sorts of past attributions—power plays, being shamed, oppressed, assaulted, or other violent mental associations. But sex and erotica are also liberating, fun, loving, spiritual, and positively and energetically healing. Men and women who take a stance on their sexuality can be termed "whore" or "prude". If a woman chooses not to have sex with someone she can be shamed or have anger projected at her, and the same happens if she chooses to have sex in socially unsanctioned contexts. (Men may also experience shaming for that situation.) She must overcome the fear, shame, and guilt and own up to who she is. Self-love is a lesson of Vesta. That requires the acceptance of her work or sexual/spiritual nature, however dark or taboo it is. Only then can she focus on her true work, what she was born to do.

When a man does not want to have sex, a woman may think there is something wrong with her. If a man says "no" for any reason, a woman should not push him—just as she expects a man to do if she says "no". There are many reasons a man may turn down sex, and it is not always what we think it is. Lifting one up while putting the other down is how the mess of the sexes (races, classes, etc.) began. A Vestal is centered within himself. If we have standards for one side we must also have standards for the other.

The goddess Vesta brings up the issues of the things you have done that you do not feel good about. She gives you the space/opportunity/lesson to bring your issues to focus/awareness. A question to ask the self: "Where did the desire come from that has shaped where I am or how I feel now?" She accepts you and your desires. You are to learn to do the same. Love yourself and change any desires that do not fit that equation.

Vesta brought me the opportunity to deal with my deep-seated angst about myself and how it affects other people. Dissolution of ego begins with humility, and forgiving those parts of yourself in order to help others. You come to terms with your own pitfalls, accepting them as they are, you accept who you are ... completely and wholly. She brings up the stuff you feel bad about and forces you to deal with it. It will continue to be a focus until you take responsibility for it and accept it as it is.

My progressed Vesta is in Scorpio, my 12th house/temple. I feel like a sexual deviant except I am not having sex. I want to have a partner, but I do not want the responsibility or any consequences that could result from the action of sex with another. I am undergoing my Pluto square Pluto currently. It is the transformation before the Uranus opposition. I have been trying to prepare myself for this coming transit. My progressed ascendant is conjunct the galactic center. It will enter Capricorn, during the Saturn/Pluto conjunction of 2020.

Nov. 7, 2019: I felt the urge coming over me. The Sun is transiting Scorpio and my 12th house. I have been pulling up the nitty-gritty of my past (Mercury Rx in Scorpio). I have been thinking about all the times I had sex even though I did not want to. I masturbated and let it all come over me. Pain, humiliation, abuse, and giving in to another's desire. I cried; and I came three times. Turning over negative past experiences while entranced in a ritual of sorts, I created more positive, empowering ones. My masculine self has staked claim to my feminine. That, in itself, is empowering. It also offers a bit of security.

Past sexual assaults have been coming up from my subconscious. In some strange way, the memories turned me on. It was painful, and it made me want to fuck. I forgave myself and the other person. Through self-stimulation, I turned it into Love, myself taking myself, again and again, taking me back into myself, transmuting trauma into purpose. This experience became a ritual. I was pulling my life force sent into the world back into myself. Self-contained, I felt sexy and powerful.

Love is the Law! We as Earthlings vibrate on the Ray of Love. While writing this book, I looked for an antonym for sexuality in the case of duality. I opened a thesaurus and found the word hate. Hate is the antonym for sexuality. I expected to find Love but found sexuality. Is hate not also the antonym for Love? Sexuality is Love!

The power of feeling sexy is the fire of our creative desire. To love and know thyself is powerful. Confidence and aligned chakras are sexy. Others recognize this and react or respond. It can be an empowering reminder to strive to be the best self by being who we are. We create our lives with power and purpose, it is work, and it takes energy to make energy.

I remember a vision I had during this process. I was on my knees, submissively, with my hands tied above my head. A Saturn-type figure stood behind me with a sickle. Was I giving into death? No. I had slight fear/resistance. Later, in my studies, I identified a possible link to

Vesta and an ancient Hindu goddess myth of Renuka and Parashurama. Renuka was beheaded and became Yellamma. (Renuka is discussed more fully at the end of the chapter *Vesta and the Other Goddesses*.) Vesta needs Saturn in her life; Saturn is discipline. He is the leader/father figure. A Vestal who made a mistake was tied up and whipped by the Pontifex Maximus. Self-control is required to focus. When one has many desires, focus becomes difficult. Saturn is there to remind her that she has only so much time to work on herself spiritually.

One often needs to retreat after an energy exchange to cleanse and refocus. The complexities of the mundane can bog a Vestal down. An initiate of Vesta, monk, nun, priest, or priestess must make time for contemplation. She needs her own sacred space, especially after being overworked.

I feel the need to join a monastery. Celibacy is hard. I lasted maybe eight months (one month per year of marriage) without another entering my temple, but I was not completely non-sexual. I did not want to be celibate, but I am loyal to my devotion. I do not see how people do it; I was so tempted! I still masturbated. I felt like a sexual wanton! I can do without, but then I crave it more. Especially at peak times, I have been awakened to my dark-nature or my primal erotic, sensual craving, Devi. I say to myself, *Close the mouth of the lion.*

Celibacy can carry different meanings. To me, it allows masturbation and means no sex with another. It does, maybe, seem to imply less sex in general. I have met some who believe masturbation is tied up with virginity and ends when one finds a partner. Meditating on this interesting concept, I opened to page 52 of the book *Astrology: Evolution and Revolution* by author/astrologer Alan Oken:

> Chastity...a tool toward greater consciousness...useful only to one schooled in conscious control of the life energies ... [energy] must be appropriately protracted for human evolution ...when consciously restrained ... the technique must be known [for proper initiation].

Celibacy (consciously imposed chastity) serves a higher purpose. It leads to greater creative power, an awareness of self, and a connection to the divine. This practice is not for everyone, nor is it the only path to divine happiness. Working with a guru or high priest/priestess is advised. In retrospect, the same concept/spirituality can be found in the highly sexed. The more one can focus sexual and creative energy, the more likely one is to reach enlightenment. Many paths lead to the same conclusion, however. It was through experiencing my own sexuality that I reached the emptiness of Shiva.

I have learned that chastity means more than what some consider virginity. Chastity is present in numerous people and ways. Chastity is faithfulness. We are chaste as long as we are faithful. One may be a religious devotee, or devoted to a cause or work ethic, or bound in a marriage or higher relationship with conscious involvement. Meditating on this vow has me pondering other vows that nuns, monks, or priests today may take. Obedience I can do; unless, however, that means asking permission for everything or giving up my autonomy. The virtue of obedience is yielding to your own will. Poverty, I could not vow to. I have been poor and economically speaking I am poor; globally speaking I am rich. I choose to live better, and I have everything I want or need. It is not poverty that is the virtue, but knowing how to be abstemious and resourceful that is the virtue of poverty.

Not every Vestal, priest or priestess/nun is celibate. A small number of Buddhist monastic sects (Nyingma Tibetan and some Zen traditions) marry and have sex. In Catholicism, a religious vow of chastity is more appropriately called celibacy(not to marry). There are also Asian traditions that practice sexual retention.

On the opposite side, imposed celibacy can lead to repression of sexuality. When repressed, sexual energy can erupt like a volcano when triggered. Anger and frustration or war and violence can ensue. Properly directed, it can be powerfully positive. Sexual energy needs expression; proper expression requires practice. Step 1 is recognizing this energy. Step 2 is using it in a reverent and constructive way. Step 3 is where the result of this energy leads—healing, creating, or sustaining. The three forms of Shakti: desire/will, knowledge, action.

I utilize many great teachings. Through my experience, I have learned that Vesta is retelling Shakti. Shakti is looking for Shiva in some form or fashion. The union is the end of duality, a oneness with God, a complete awareness of all that is, was, and will be. Holding focus and having holy intent and devotion is to honor Vesta.

Although Vestals enter into the divine marriage, Vesta is not mentioned much in connection with married women. Vesta is the domestic goddess, as are many married women. Marriage is very Vestal; vows endure, they enter into a new family. When I think of the divine marriage, I think of Shiva and Shakti. Shakti craves her Shiva as Shiva craves his Shakti. Sometimes they separate, and Shakti goes her way. She often returns to her God as another goddess and marries him again in a different form. It is Vesta/Shakti who keeps the flames alive.

At the beginning of my Vesta journey, my will became writing this book. Challenges, obstacles, distractions, and adversaries crossed my path; it was part of my teaching and training. My goal is a work of focused dedication. It was not easy. Although, many days on the periphery with Vesta, I manage to put my devotion into focusing my will. Inner spiritual work had to transpire. Purify and discipline focus. What is genuine, what belongs, and what does not?

RACHEL MCCABE
WINTER 2021

Part 1
History and Holiness

The Beginnings of Vesta

> *I am a biotheist and a heyoka. I was Hindu in a past life. Nature is my establishment. I am Lady of the woods and nymph of the sacred waters. I believe in the Universal Source, The Great Spirit, the infinite Shiva, The God/Goddess unity. My religion is Love, the Earth, the stars, and the present moment.*

I am not sure if I am the right person to be writing a book on the Virgin Goddess, or the kind, beautiful mind/body soundness of her representation, the Vestal Virgins ... I certainly do not nominate myself as such. But I am writing the book just the same. I would like to take you through a journey. One beginning with now, back through the patriarchy, back to the matriarchy, and into the woods where it all began.

There is a reason for the essential secrecy of Vesta. Some secrets must be kept. I share many secrets in this book, but keep most to myself. My experience with Vesta is deep and very personal. I did want to add it all in this book, but Vesta is very self-contained. She is often hidden away from society, as her very nature is sacred or taboo. The taboo is like the moon in its many phases and bright or dark faces. Sometimes they are revealed. There are always pieces hidden. As you search, the more it becomes visible or obscure depending on how and when you view it. One must sort through the mess of interpretations and misinterpretations. You find what works for you, and you discard what does not. The duty of the Vestals is Purification. When one finds an issue, one works through it or works to remove it.

The original Roman Vesta is a fire and household goddess. The home is the temple, and the hearth is the altar. Vesta is not just the sacred fire of the oven but the heart of the fire. She is the space that encompasses all. She holds the passion that lies within.

Cooking and cleaning are sacred. How we cleanse, the nutrients we take in, and how we adorn ourselves matter to Vesta. Hard work is her forte. She represents our sacramental services to our physical needs like food, shelter, sex, clothing, and spirit (fire, earth, water, and air). She is our sacred space (ether).

The cult of Vesta during ancient Rome was the height of her worship, but she has been around much longer and is still relevant today. Before the Roman Vestals, there were oracles, nymphs, and temple priestesses. These priests and priestesses still exist today in many forms. They live in the sacred homes, monasteries and temples, convents, or other ministries of spirit/god/goddess; but also in the home itself. We are all the priests or priestesses of our home.

Today's monks/nuns or priests/priestesses are usually on the path of renunciation or the practice of non-attachment. The belief is to give up everything to commune with God/Goddess, the Christ, higher self, or universe. Stories of living nuns reveal that each is uniquely diverse. Their lives relate to Vesta or the Vestal Virgins, but they are human just like everyone else.

Catholic nuns today are often more feminist than they were before. They may not hold as much power as they did in the time of the Vestal or before the patriarchy, but the punishment for breaking vows is not as severe today as it was during the height of the Roman Vestal era. Vestals are human, and vows tested. Not everyone passes the test the first time.

The matriarchy once ruled the world. Before biology was known women were worshipped as the goddess or the creator. From them comes life. They owned themselves. One with the earth, they were capable of profound healing. Temple priestesses held the highest spiritual authority. These women were whole in themselves and their sexuality was celebrated.

Later, these priestesses became subject to the patriarchy and were made dependent upon the hierarchy of men. Maybe that was the biggest reason behind the Vestal cult: though the Vestals were under the authority of the state and/or Emperor, they were whole unto themselves. Even the patriarchy recognized the importance of an independent woman's voice concerning the state. Before this time, however, priestesses and women were allowed to take care of themselves. They had jobs of their own and did not require the authority of men, although they would gladly accept an exchange or donation for their craft.

Men have also been hurt by the patriarchy. They are required to be the head of household, breadwinner, hard and unwavering, stifling emotions, soldier, or tough guy. They shoulder the most responsibility when it comes to leadership because of the patriarchy. Women can lead, and some men welcome it, but the patriarchy or modern society does not accept it. There are those who hold tight to what they know and do not want to lose control of their positions.

My natal Vesta is conjunct my natal Pluto so of course I am more sexual in my spirituality, but I believe Vesta's sexuality is "occult" or hidden. Vesta was the Roman form of the Greek goddess Hestia. The ancient Greeks believed that everyone was bisexual to some extent. Suggesting Hestia as devoid of sexuality is false; Hestia's fire burns in every home. I am not trying to sexualize Vesta, but I am understanding of her nature and that of my own.

Every one of us has a destiny to fulfill. People with Vesta prominent in their birth chart sometimes have a hard time understanding this concept, and they surrender to the many needs of others. They may be trapped in one focus and miss the point. They must develop their own-will and path.

As a wife and mother, I understand the importance of leadership and establishing boundaries. If you do not practice asserting your will in the family, you will be run over and taken advantage of, which is all too often normal for the "good wife" in the world of the patriarchy. However, Hestia rules the home. She controls the fire within, intuition, and the psyche of one's self. She is known as the maid of the house, cook, seamstress, and the preserver of what is.

Other people's desires affect Vestals, especially in the family/those closest to them. They must hold, or learn to hold, their own will. Whether or not their will is to be bound or free is up to the individual. However, most often, Vesta will give up her position for security. Vesta in Libra, for example, may have a hard time making decisions and, therefore, may leave the decision-making up to another.

Vestals may be the caretakers and helpers in their communities. They are involved in politics, devoting themselves to expanding the views of others. They are the scribes of historical events. They hold the sacred space needed to feel safe. Because Vestals tend to give more than they receive, the less informed may have their giving natures taken for granted. This may cause them to seek some sort of cloister as an escape from the impurities of the world.

Vesta, at her best, grants Vestals a certain amount of intimacy with others without the responsibility for the life of the other. She serves, but not necessarily a husband or children. A servant to the divine will, she takes care of the community while still establishing a private or divine life of her own. Often, her work is her divine life.

We know only a fraction about the Vestal Virgins of ancient Rome. What we do know is that they were expected to be pure and abstain from sexual intercourse with men. The scholars of the time painted Rome as pure and incorruptible; the unclean were cast away from society. Romans were very superstitious. If they prayed to the wrong god, if the fire went out, or if a Vestal broke her vows, it was a bad omen and a possible destroyer of Rome. If the fire was to go out, the Vestals were to start it again from the purest source: the Sun. The Pontifex Maximus would use a magnifying glass to concentrate the Sun's fire. We also find references to a fire-stick, or a torch that lights the eternal flame. Often, this sacred flame was passed out to light the fires of the Roman hearths, and coals were carried with them when they traveled away from their home/hearth. The Sun's energy concentrated into a usable source has now re-established itself as the cleanest, most reusable resource.

Vesta is the asteroid of solitude, and a Vestal will need to spend a lot of time alone, especially when working on projects. Virgo, Vesta's ruler, is known as the "hermit of the zodiac". Tunnel vision, or not seeing the forests for the trees, is a side-effect of Virgo and Vesta. They can become so involved in their work that others may see them as rude as their tunnel vision seems to block others out. However, like Virgo, Vesta is very service-oriented and wants to serve her community.

A Vestal can get into trouble if she becomes off-balance and overextends herself. Having too many irons in the fire can burn out the fire. She must not sacrifice herself by having too much to do. By focusing (Vesta), we will accomplish what we set out to do in this life. If we ignore her, we suffer. It takes work, voice, and dedication to perform our objectives. Sometimes the world can become too much, and Vesta needs to retreat from time to time to recharge her energy, focus/mind, body.

When one meets another with a radiating kundalini/life force, the energy can be intoxicating. But if the devotion is not present, Vesta tends to her fire alone. When awakened, she prefers real, passionate love over transient lust. She keeps the partnerships alive when impassioned. It is difficult for her to end the idea of the partnership if that has been her devotion, whether that devotion belongs to deity or master or self or creation. She must obey her vows, or she may be buried alive by dirty emotions, guilt, or shame; she must retreat into herself when a partnership is formed or broken. Time spent alone should be the focus at those times. What are the lessons? Listen to the goddess within. She has much to teach you.

Purity: To be wholly and completely pure. Unless you see everything as pure, nothing is pure. What is pure? Energy is pure. The thought is that fire is pure. Is it? What fire burns is rarely pure. Fire is a purifying agent. Fire destroys everything; only the pure remain. In alchemy, you remove the dross or burn the impure away from the pure. Sexual energy is pure, a sacred fire; and orgasm is pure, organic energy. I have linked Vesta with explosions, energy, and fuel of many sorts.

Be aware of black magic and your seductive powers. Vestals may tend to give others what they seek, sometimes at the expense of their own. Like fire, she is a shapeshifter. A Vestal becomes what they need her to be. Vesta is selective, however. Vesta protects initiates from wild winds and the seduction of the sorcerer.

A Vestal creates the space needed to do her work. She is the fire, tamer, controller, and extinguisher. Dissolution of the Ego is just one of many deaths a Vestal will have to accept in her life. Saturn is the father of Vesta, after all. Vesta requires his discipline.

Being submissive to the universe is being dominant in human relationships and situations. If you act on the decree of the universe, then the river flows for you and through you. You know you are not the source but a fountain of the well-spring from which the living waters flow.

No expectations. No comfort zone. You do not know what is going to happen. Trust in the universe. The truth is erotic.

To be wanted and desired is a powerful thing. To give in to the dis-ire of another can be a weakness. It may have psychological, emotional, or physical effects, but to give in to the desires of your God/Goddess, highest self, the Universe, or Master is the ultimate experience. There is no regret, it is not a weakness, and it takes strength and trust to surrender.

One cannot be solely devoted when there is another to be devoted to, however. A virgin is sovereign. Loss of virginity is loss of sovereignty because most people who engage in sex are relationship-bound or vice-versa. One identifies how relationships are supposed to be between a man and a woman at an early age. How you see your parents treat each other, how society treats man and woman, and the first relationships we develop with the opposite sex determines how our relationships are affected throughout our lives. If someone is abused or sees their parent mistreated, they might believe that is how relationships are.

Sometimes we grow out of those beliefs, and sometimes we do not. Traumatic experiences can cause us to stay stuck in the mindset of the time it happened. That is why some victims cannot seem to escape their victimhood and continue to put themselves in similar situations because they do not know any better. They may not understand that victimhood is not normal, and they have a choice in the matter. Initially, by reliving the act, one can change how one reacts.

Through the research I have found on kundalini rising, it is a very personal experience. I have not yet found someone who experienced kundalini rise while engaged in intercourse with another human being, but the energy can be tapped into again after the initial experience with or without a partner. When we clear what is blocking, our life-energy is allowed to flow freely throughout the body.

Vesta has a way of bringing up these matters so that we can deal with them. Invoking her presence means we are opening ourselves to healing and protection during that time of transition. To experience the higher connection with the divine, we have to allow the unknown to occur.

Norma Jean Mortensen/Baker (Marilyn Monroe) has a grand trine, Vesta with Mars and Saturn. She has Saturn in Scorpio in her 4th house. Her home life was unsettling; her mother was unable to care for her due to health problems. Marilyn endured nine or more foster homes. She may have been an abused child, held in that age; some say Norma was like a little girl in real life. She may have used this candid act as a coping mechanism she developed at an early age.

Like the goddess herself, the roles Marilyn played in movies brought out many traits of her personality. She has Chiron on her MC; acting healed her and wounded her. She tried to keep her dark feminine hidden. Lilith is in her 12th house/temple.

Norma Jean was known as a "shining flame" on stage. Vesta in the 12th house/temple is opposite her South Node in her 6th house/temple, which shows she was comfortable expressing her sexuality through her work. Chiron is square Pallas and conjunct her MC. She may have been too hurt to fight for a higher place in Hollywood. Perhaps she looked for a partner to help get her "there". She feared having children because of inherited sexual and mental health problems—not wanting to pass them onto her children. (Also, Vesta in the 12th house/temple is the least likely to want or to have children.) She enjoyed her private life. Dreams and fantasies were her sacred space.

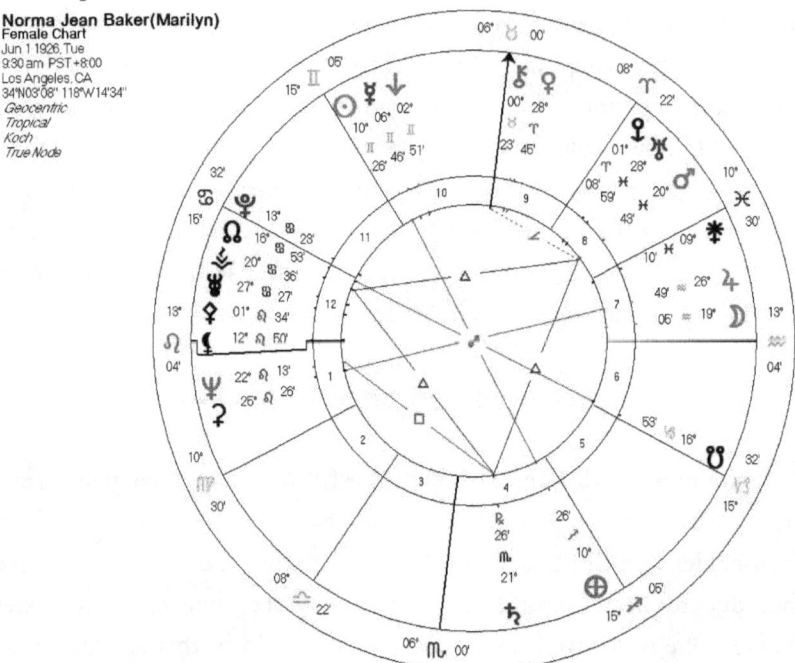

Hugh Hefner, the creator of Playboy magazine, was also very Vestal. I did not know the two (Hugh and Marilyn) were connected until I did the research. It seems, although the two never actually met, they are strangely connected in life and death. In 1949, Norma Jean Baker did a nude calendar shoot under a fake name (Marilyn Monroe). She was under financial distress and needed the money. In 1953, Hugh Hefner published the first issue of Playboy featuring "Marilyn Monroe" from that calendar shoot. The issue sold out! Over 50,000 copies were bought in the first week, which was a lot in the 1950s.

Ms. Baker did not consent to Hugh using her pictures in the magazine, nor did she ever receive compensation for their usage. But I think they both made each other's fame; her photos/his magazine. For a hefty price, he bought the crypt next to hers in Westwood Village Memorial Park Cemetery where they lie together "for eternity".

Hugh Hefner was an activist. Sexual liberation and freedom of expression were very important to him. He fought and donated money for First Amendment rights(freedom to be ourselves), animal rescue, cinematic arts, anti-vaccine campaigns, same-sex marriage, and the restoration of the Hollywood sign. His oldest daughter created the Hugh M. Hefner First Amendment Award, "to honor individuals who have made significant contributions in the vital effort to protect and enhance First Amendment rights for Americans."

With Vesta, Pallas, Pluto, and the North Node in the 10th house he was a businessman. He lived the *bon vivant* life, lavish luxury at its finest (Cancer 10th house, and Ceres and Neptune in Leo, 11th house). With Vesta in Cancer, he was devoted to his creature comforts and his home. His Playboy Mansion is known worldwide. With Virgo rising, he was serious about his service and dedicated to sexual liberation. Hef's voice and activism were carried and emphasized throughout many different films and television shows over many years.

When I think of a man who has Vesta prominent in his chart, I think of Hugh Hefner. Men with Vesta prominent are often surrounded by women. A true playboy that loves women and their causes! His work is his sacred path.

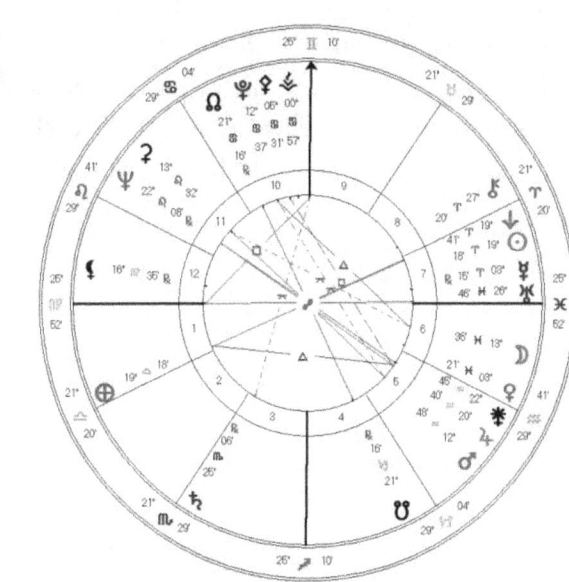

The Greek Goddess Hestia

We join spokes together on a wheel,
But it is the center hole,
That makes the wagon move.
We shape clay into a pot,
But it is the emptiness inside,
That holds whatever we want.
We hammer wood for a house,
But it is the inner space,
That makes it livable.
We work with being,
But non-being,
Is the thing we use.
- Lao-Tzu.

To honor Vesta is to honor Hestia. Hestia is a threshold goddess; she provides sanctuary to the weary traveler and the local artist. Her devotees take care of the home and hearth—that is, they do the cooking and cleaning, among other things. These small acts of service are sacred to the goddess. She is our reminder of the sacredness of the simple things in life. To embrace the service(s) you provide is divine. Keeping the sacred spaces clean allows for a clear mind and body. Creative and destructive acts, such as cooking and cleaning, provide opportunities to live in the present. She teaches the joy of the sacred inner space.

I circle my hearth from without
And I focus the work of my hands.
I circle my hearth from within
And I focus the work of my heart.
Every work of my hands is a victory won,
Every thing that I do is another thing done.
-Modern Neo-Pagan chant for Hestia

There would be no feasts without Hestia. She received the first and the last offerings of the festivity or daily meal, ensuring her eternal place among humanity. We cannot live without the sustenance she provides. Every city in Greece had a public hearth whose fire was to never burn out. We light candles for many celebrations and times of remembrance. Hestia is the reason the candles are to stay lit. Hestia is warmth and nourishment on a soul level; every newborn was ritualized and sanctified around the goddess Hestia and her hearth.

Archetypically, she is a goddess of architecture. Hestia embodies how the house is built up from the foundation—not only physically built, but spiritually built. Cronos (Saturn), her father, rules foundations. She works above and within. She is the sturdy structure and the keeper of the internal/eternal.

Hestia was often not personified; she was often shown only as a living flame. She did not take part in the family dramas of the other Olympians. Although Hestia is often found where the god Hermes is mentioned, they were not consorts. Hermes is the trickster, traveler, and the messenger of the gods. As a psychopomp, he is known to lead mortals into the underworld (and, sometimes, out). Hermes is Mercury, ruler of communications.

Hestia and Hermes, threshold gods, dwell at the doorway to becoming. Whichever way you choose, they are there to help you through transition. It is in times of change, upheaval, or confusion that we encounter them. It seems that at these times, like the dark night of the soul, we are most connected to the divine.

These friends, Hermes and Hestia, meet you at the gateway. A loss of something important to us can create liminality, a space that is between spaces, neither one thing nor the other. Liminality stems from the Latin word *limen*, a threshold. This "liminality" often occurs through major life transits and changes, such as Saturn returns and midlife crises. Change is happening no matter how much we want it or not; we can no longer be who we were in the past. Hermes is spiritual change on the outside, and Hestia is spiritual change on the inner realms. When I think of these two together, I think of the same ends of two magnets coming together until stilled; space lies in-between. Resistance holds space/focus. Hermes is swift outer action that guides and brings messages. Hestia protects, informs, and helps in meditation and contemplation. Hermes is the god of social society; he is the trickster, the thief, and the fast communicator. Hestia is the goddess of the inner society; often, she sacrifices the outer exchange for a happy home. She is the passion and process.

There are no known temples found for the Greek goddess Hestia. The personal center, the hearth of the home, the heart-of-the-city, and the center-of-the-Earth are her temples. Her acts and rituals may go largely unacknowledged as they are simple and a part of everyday life. Each action is a spiritual ritual, acknowledged or not. Her ritual is her work. She is centered in her temple wherever she is. The soul is a place, her sacred center, her home.

Hermes/Mercury is androgynous and connects to the gods and humanity. Bringing messages, s/he interprets them how s/he sees fit. Hestia enjoys the same gatherings as Mercury. Hermes brings the memorandum, whether it is true, mixed up, or outright lies. Hestia is the protector of the official records and often speaks up when the conversation is uncentered. She knows that many things are at stake and invests herself in those communications. She purifies the message.

Hestia gave up her seat to Dionysus when he demanded to be seated with the gods, the Twelve Olympians. She took her place, the interior space of the throne room. At the center of the throne room sat the sacred hearth of eternal light. She chose to keep the flame alight. Hestia, in her kindness, chooses duty over ecstasy.

Though Hestia may be simple in execution, her rituals take place in the privacy of home and hearth and sometimes at the heart-of-the-community. Hestia remains neutral in conflict or war. Being centered in herself, she is the local diplomat. Hestia is a visionary; she is a guide and noticed in dream space. We can be present in dream time, and astral projection comes easily to those who cross the threshold.

Hestia is involved in the psyche. Hestia/Vesta showed me my different paths, depending on which I chose. It did not look bleak, and the Sun was shining in the vision she provided me. But it was uncertain. Hestia, stuck in her ways, has no movement on her own. I am happy in my life, of writing, art, pottery making, and children. I did not want to change that. That life, however, comes with the duties of cooking, cleaning, and caring for others. Others' demands, often taking presence above one's own.

The goddess revealed things to me in dreams and in real-time. Before there was even a hint of separation, I dreamt of a very dark night. The courts were involved, and we had to move because my husband was the accused. We, my children and I, stayed by him in the dream. We were with him when the Sun rose after the long night.

It happened just as my dream predicted it. During that dark time of separation, I had more premonition dreams that also included the fate of other people. Hestia showed me what was real and what was not, what belonged to me and what did not, and hidden desires that may never happen but must rise to the surface. Through dreams and visions, I communicate with the goddess of the eternal flame, my inner core.

The Myths and Origins of Vesta

"There is no fixity in mythical concepts: they can come into being, alter, disintegrate, disappear completely". - Roland Barthes

Vesta's mythology begins with Hestia, the Greek goddess of the hearth. The Romans gathered many ideas from the Greeks and other traveling people, such as deities and architecture (also ruled by Hestia) and made them their own. Vesta was the eldest child of Kronos (Saturn, who ate his children) and Rhea (Ops). She was, therefore, the first to be swallowed up by Saturn and the last to be reborn. She is both youngest and oldest of her brothers and sisters: Ceres, Jupiter, Juno, Neptune, and Pluto (Roman); Demeter, Zeus, Hera, Poseidon, and Hades (Greek).

Vesta is the Roman equivalent of the Greek goddess Hestia. According to Plato, her name means "the essence of things", but there are many etymologies for Vesta and Hestia. Scholars generally agree that her name descends from an old word for "hearth", descended from an even older word meaning "to burn".

Hestia/Vesta is the most anonymous of the Greco-Roman goddesses. The Gods Poseidon/Neptune and Apollo battled for her hand, but hating the division, she rejected them both, preferring to stay in her power as a virgin. Her brother, Zeus/Jupiter, allowed her to stay in his home, where she happily attended his home and hearth in return. Zeus/Jupiter granted her the honor of presiding over all sacrifices. She was the goddess that opened and closed each ritual of the gods, and brought the purifying agent to each rite. Vesta is the first and the last, always honored before and after the feast. She is the essence of domestic bliss.

Vesta is not fond of discord. She was part of the original 12 Olympians, but gave up her seat to Dionysus/Bacchus, the youngest son of Zeus/Jupiter, to avoid conflict and possibly civil war. She dedicated herself to attending the sacred flame rather than family controversy and drama.

Dionysus, taking the seat on the side of the goddesses, suggests a gender change. Being of Greek origin, of course, he is bisexual and many stories portray him as androgynous. God/goddess of wine, s/he was known for their wild, intoxicating parties.

Romulus and Remus

Romulus and Remus, the founders of Rome, were said to be conceived from a mystic disembodied phallus. In the Aeneid, by Virgil, their mother was the Vestal Virgin Rhea Silvia, and their father was the god of war himself, Mars. The Roman version of the Romulus and Remus, written much later, was changed to a longer exaltation of Rome and its attributes.

The phallus came from the sacred hearth of Vesta. In Plutarch's story, King Tarchetius of Alba was advised by the Oracle of Tethys in Etrusca (Tuscany) to present the phallus to a virgin so that she could have sex with it. He called on his daughter, who refused and sent her handmaiden, who also refused. King Tarchetius imprisoned both handmaiden and daughter for their disobedience, and threatened to kill them. Vesta appeared, through a dream-vision, to the king. As protector of children and virgins, she forbade him from committing such a crime.

In their chains, the king ordered both handmaiden and princess to sew a silk web. When they finished the project, he said they could marry. Each night while they slept, by order of the king, their work unraveled. When the handmaiden gave birth to twins, King Tarchetius ordered his subordinate Teratius to destroy them. Teratius laid the babes by the shore of the rising Tiber river, but a she-wolf found them and nursed them. A woodpecker brought them fruit and nuts. The twins of Rome, discovered by a cow-herder, were brought up by him and his wife (possibly the Lupoe). The she-wolf or Lupoe (loose woman) and the woodpecker are sacred to the god Mars and to Rome.

Figure 1: *Capitoline She-wolf (Lupa capitolina) at the Musei (museum) on Capitoline Hill in Rome, Italy. To learn more about the ancient Vestals, visit their home in Rome. I was fortunate to visit Rome as a young child. There are many museums, ruins, and artifacts to explore. One rememberable artifact is the wolf mother statue or Lupa Capitolina.*

Perseus

The story of Romulus and Remus has a striking similarity to the Greek mythology of Perseus. He was the son of Zeus and his mother was Danaë, the daughter of Acrisius, king of Argos. Acrisius visited the Oracle to inquire about having sons. The Oracle told him that he would have none, but his daughter would have a son. She said Danaë would betray him and her son would overthrow him. Acrisius was angered by this and locked Danaë in an underground chamber.

Danaë was a devotee and spent her isolation praying to the gods. She was very beautiful, which brought the attention of Zeus. He transformed into a golden shower to enter her cell, and Danaë became pregnant. At the sound of a baby crying, her guards alerted the king. Acrisius unlocked her door to find her holding a babe. She said, "His name is Perseus," which means avenger or destroyer.

Since the gods frown on murdering one's own offspring, Acrisius nailed them both in a wooden box and set them out to sea. Danaë prayed to the gods, who smiled on them; providing a safe journey, light rain to drink, and small fish to eat. They landed on the shore of Seriphos, an island east of Argos, where they were found and presented to the king of Seriphos, Polydectes, who granted them asylum and sent them to live in the Temple of Athena. King Polydectes desired to marry Danaë, but she thwarted all of his advances.

Numa

A story by the Greek Diocles of Peparethus, says that King Numitor had a daughter and made her a Vestal. She was bound to live as a single maiden for her whole life. Her name was Ilia, Rhea, or Silvia. Not long after entering the vows of Vesta, they learned she was pregnant. Her sister talked their father, the king, out of the horrible demise that would have been leveled on Ilia for her breaking of the sacred vows. Instead, Ilia was put in solitary confinement. She gave birth to two strong, healthy, boys to which the story continues much like the first.

Other stories are in line with the above. More on Romulus can be found in Livy's *The History of Rome*, Dionysius of Halicarnassus' *Roman Antiquities*, Ovid's epic poem *Fasti*, Cassius Dio's *History of the Romans*, and Plutarch's *Life of Romulus*.

Some say it was Numa's palace where the phallus first appeared in the hearth of Vesta. Ocresia, a handmaiden, being the first to see it, was chosen for consummation. Vulcan appeared, and she disappeared until she gave birth to Servius Tullius. Sevius means "son of servant", and Tullius means "one who leads". Virgo is the virgin and the servant of the astrological signs.

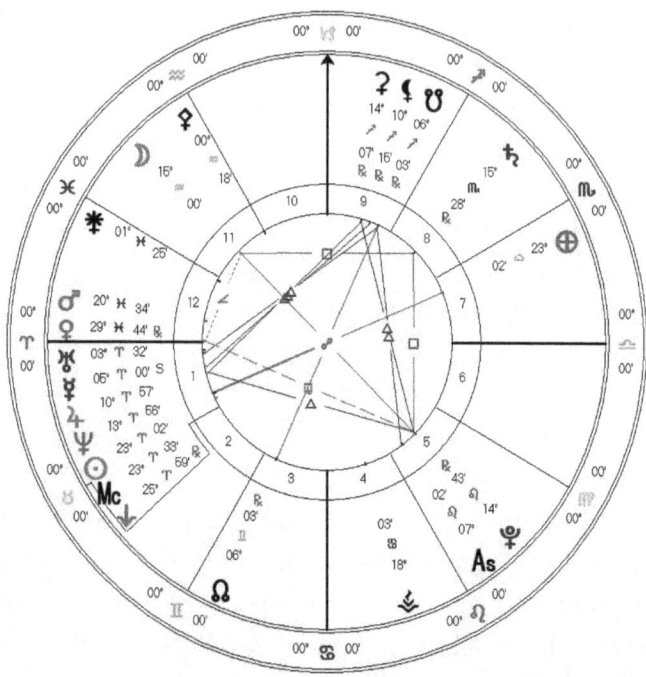

Numa Pompilius, the second king of Rome, was an astrologer and reunification was his goal. He was born on the day of the founding of Rome, April 21, 753 BC. It was written in the stars that he should be king, and the people approved of him. He sought to teach the Roman people peace instead of war. His religion taught that the home and the place of goods were the sacred temples, so every home in Rome became temple space of Vesta.[1]

Numa was the initiator of the Roman Vesta cult and hand-picked four Vestals. Four is the number of the foundation; they came together on the foundation of sisterhood. The Vestal Virgins were the fair and noble guardians of Rome. Beautiful in body and mind, the young girls were Gegania, Verania, Canuleia, and Tarpein. Although the Vesta cult predates Etruscan culture (about 900 BC), they were the first Vestals of Numa's Rome.

---

[1] http://www.novaroma.org/nr/Numa_tradition

Numa built the temple Jupiter Optimums Maximus which the Vestal Virgins attended on Capitoline Hill. Next to the Temple of Vesta, home of the sacred fire, Numa built the Atrium Vestae, a garden and Atrium with two pools surrounded by a portico, a porch with columns supporting a roof.

The Emperor's Palace (Domus Tiberiana), built next to the Atrium opposite the Casa delle Vestali, is a three-story, fifty-room palace. The House of Vestals is where the Vestals resided. Its location is at the foot of Palatine Hill, between the Temple of Vesta, and the palace, Domus Tiberiana in the Roman Forum.

Figure 2: *Photo of the Temple of Vesta in the Roman Forum.*

The temple of Vesta has been damaged and rebuilt many times. Another temple on the acropolis of Tivoil may be a better representative of what the temple looked like. Built on the model of the ancient hearth, the temple was round, open to the sky, and the hearth in the center. There is controversy about whether the temple of Tivoil is actually a temple of Vesta, but the concept is similar. The temple of Vesta in Rome was built around the 7th century BC and the temple in Tivoil was built around the first century BC.

Hestia, being the goddess of architecture, was the inspiration of the building for the divine. The temple of Jupiter was also dedicated to his wife Juno and daughter Minerva (Athena). Jupiter was Numa's deity. Numa's reign was said to be the oldest, purest, and most reverent of Roman cults. His sacrifices to the gods, Plutarch wrote, "were not celebrated with effusion of blood, but consisted of flour, wine, and the least costly offerings." It was the beginning of puritan Rome.

Numa, himself, was severely disciplined and expected the same of his Vestals. His natal Moon and Pluto are in a T-square with Saturn, and he has a stellium of planets in Aries including his Sun. Numa also created the cult of Mars, Jupiter, Minerva, and Terminus the "God of Boundaries" (erecting phalli to set property lines and landmarks). After Rome became a peaceful state, his goal, Numa closed the doors of the temple, never to be opened again until after his reign. With Vesta in Cancer, his sacred place was in his home.

In myth or legend, Numa was said to have sought counsel from Egoria, the nymph of the bubbling spring. She was a priestess of the Moon goddess Diana. It was she who taught him the gentle, soothing ways of water, the occult, and how to govern or manipulate the people for the good of all. At the death of Numa, she was most distraught. Her tears ran so deep, the goddess transformed the priestess into a fountain of ever-flowing water or spring of wisdom. This spring is where many Vestals have found inspiration. It is said Numa passed this wisdom onto the Vestal Virgins. His wisdom likely included the occult, goddess initiation, and astrology.

Numa's books from the teachings of the nymph Egoria and the Muses were kept only for priests (Flamines, Pontifices, Salii, and Fetiales). He wrote a series of sacred books and was buried with them and his seals. The books were burned by the Victimarii around 273 BC the year his tomb was uncovered.

Numa witnessed fire as pure and uncorrupted and therefore wanted the same for the Vestals. He named himself High Priest, Pontifex Maximus, of the guardians of the sacred fire. If the fire were to go out accidentally instead of through ritual extinction, a Vestal was blamed and punished. The high priest would whip them and reignite the flame, using a magnifying glass to concentrate the Sun's rays into igniting a fire stick. The fire stick was inserted into the hearth for re-ignition of the sacred flame.

He died in the year 673 BC. Numa's tomb, with seven books in Latin on Roman law and seven books in Greek on Greek philosophy, were discovered about 400 years later. Priest decided not to reveal these books to the public and they were said to have been burned.

The Roman Vesta

Vesta is the most sacred goddess of Rome. Her flame, through which she operates, gave birth to the Roman foundation. Through her, generation after generation of the human race thrives. She is the creation, the virgin, and the mother. Every Roman home has a hearth, and every member of the household gave sacrifice to Vesta. The fireplace is a place of refuge and was the central element, and the sacred flame was kept alive and inviolable. Although not devoid of sex, the Romans considered Vesta perfect for her integrity and immortality. She is the representation of the Virgin Mother of Rome.

The Roman Goddess, Vesta, originated from Alba Longa and is a part of the Penates or Trojan gods established from the Greek tradition. She was first known as Vesta Illiaca or Vesta of Troy. Vesta, Hestia in Greek, of Troy, was possibly related to Pallas or Minerva. Made in the image of the goddess, the Palladium was a magical object that protected the city. Taken from Troy, it was one kept among the sacred relics in the Roman Vestal temple. Another of her many names includes Diva Palatua. She was also known to serve the temples of Jupiter and Mars.

In the story or myth, the Greek Athena and Pallas, or the Roman Minerva and Pallas were friends and practiced combat. While sparring, Minerva accidentally killed Pallas due to an influence by Zeus. She then carved the Palladium to look like her friend. She presented it to Zeus and he threw it to Earth. It landed in the hands of a man praying for a sign in the location of Troy before it was built. As long as it remained inside the city walls, Troy would never fall. The Greeks, learning this, stole the Palladium. Somehow it ended up in Roman hands and became a *pignora Imperii* or sacred relic of Rome. The Vestals were known to keep the Palladium safe in their possession, hidden in their storehouse of pots; they would ceremonially wash it in the Tiber river or flowing water once a year.

The health of Rome was dependent on the virtue of the Vestals. Shedding the blood of a Vestal Virgin was prohibited, even to kill her. If she broke her vow of chastity, she was to be buried alive, entombed with a ration of wine, milk, water, bread, and oil for a lamp. Her lover, if found, was whipped to death.

Vestals were vulnerable to accusations. The Vestal Tuccia was falsely accused of breaking her chastity vow and was saved by an intervention of the goddess. Vesta enabled her to carry water in a sieve from the Tiber river back to the temple where Tuccia proclaimed her innocence. Others were not so lucky.

(The romantic in me may suggest that the burial tomb was an escape. It was located outside of the city and loaded with provisions, enough to carry. A Vestal may have wished to leave the temple for whatever reason. With the help of a friend or lover, she was able to escape. But that is a fringe theory, as we may never know.)

The chief duty of the Vestal was to attend to the sacred fire. If the fire went out, the Vestal on duty would be held accountable. The Vestal fire in ancient times, if extinguished unceremoniously, meant the fall of Rome. The Vestal was not only accused of negligence but promiscuity.

According to recorded Roman history, the Vestals' most important job was storing and preserving food. They harvested grain and processed salt, and pulverized both using mortar or mill. They also made bread and brine and may have fermented the wine. They created vessels or pots to store the harvest; therefore, Vestals were likely trained in pottery making. These pots stored foodstuff, and they were also used to break down the salt for the brine. They would seal unrefined salt inside a pot and fire it, then chisel the pot open to release the salt for brine making. The Palladium was said to be in one of them, hidden in the storeroom.

A variety of different pottery and unique burial practices have been documented finds in the area of the Tiber River. People from all over migrated to the area for agriculture. *Villanorani*, or traders from Greece, largely influenced Rome. Cremation burials and underground storage shelters for food came from the knowledge of the travelers.

Priapus

In Ovid's *Fasti*, there is a feast attended by Priapus, along with other gods, satyrs, nymphs, and divinities. Vesta/Hestia lay carelessly asleep after imbuing too much wine. Priapus came across the sleeping goddess and desired to defile her, but an uninvited donkey brayed. Vesta awoke with a start, and Priapus lost his erection. Vesta escaped, and the donkey was bludgeoned to death by Priapus and his prodigious penis. In a similar story, Priapus chased the nymph Lotis. She transformed into the Lotus tree (*Ziziphus lotus*, related to the jujube), and anyone who ate of the tree would forget where they came from and would not return to their place of origin, preferring isolation.[2]

---

[2] GreekMythology.com, The Editors of Website. "Priapus". GreekMythology.com Website, 09 Apr. 2021, https://www.greekmythology.com/Other_Gods/Minor_Gods/Priapus/priapus.html. Accessed 30 July 2021.

Priapus is the son of Aphrodite and Dionysus (some say Hermes, Zeus, or Pan), and he represents the male procreative power. *Priapism*, from the name Priapus, is a medical condition resulting in an unexplained permanent erection. Priapus was cursed by the goddess Hera while still in Aphrodite's womb, due to an egotistical battle over who was the fairest (refer to Eris and the Golden Apple). Hera cursed him with impotence and a disgusting demeanor. A patron of shepherds and seamen, he was a phallic god known to run with Pan and the satyrs.

Figure 3: Bronze statuette possibly of the Roman fertility god Priapus, made in two parts (shown here in assembled and disassembled forms). This statuette has been dated to the late 1st century C.E. It was found in Rivery, in Picardy, France in 1771 and is the oldest Gallo-Roman object in the collection of the Museum of Picardy. This figurine represents the deity clothed in a "cuculus", a Gallic coat with hood, and maybe an example of the Genii cucullati. This upper section is detachable and conceals a phallus.

Priapus was not permitted to live with the gods and was cast to the Earth; he had no temples and was mostly worshiped in the home or used for humorous pornography. Depicted as a man with a large, permanent erection or a man with a penis for a head, he is the god of gardening, livestock, and male potency. He protected bees and was seen in their swarms, and worshipers erected phalli on hillsides for him. Asses were sacrificed to him, and offerings of fish, wine, fruit, vegetables, and other fertility offerings like flowers, honey, and grain. He was considered good luck (*fatmir*); although a figure of fun, he abated the evil eye.

Priapus was one of the navigational guides among ancient merchant ships; his phalluses were found among shipwrecks and on shores besides dangerous passages in the seas. The ancient Greeks believed the phallus has a mind of its own, often controlling the man to whom it belongs—possessive and territorial, and therefore Priapus was also known to protect property boundaries. Like a river or county line Priapus, or an erect phallus separates ownership.

Although the Greeks, and many people today, agree that the penis has a mind of its own, self-control can be taught and learned. Vesta teaches self-control. She will also test you on it! Boundaries connected to Vesta, daughter of Saturn, teach self-control.

The Vestals in History and the Present

> *"They're youthful and have an interior life. They're powerful women who went through a great transformation and liberated themselves."*
> -Marv Davidov

The Vestal Virgins of Rome

Vestal Virgins were initiated around six years of age. Some say it was an honor for the chosen, and some say they may have been forced into it. Not much was said for what these children needed to learn, but apparently it was best to learn it young. Later, six Vestals were chosen from a lottery of 20 girls drawn from noble families. The girls had to be pure in body and mind. Once initiated, they were to serve for 30 years.

The height of the Vestals was during classical Rome. The state sponsored their education, housing, and well-being as long as they resided in the house of Vesta. They were above the patriarchal power system and nearly above the law; independent and not owned by a husband, their family of origin, or suffered to bear children. Although they had to follow strict guidelines or face extreme punishment, they had more rights than other women. The Vestals held important documents of men, including last wills and testaments. Their word was considered pure and uncorrupt, and all things concerning Vestals were shielded from the impure or unholy.

Once a Vestal became initiated, she spent the first ten years training, then ten years administering rites, and the last ten teaching new initiates/Vestals. The Emperor or Pontifex Maximus had strict rules in which the Vestals were to follow or face extreme punishment, up to and including death. He ruled over them, and they could not speak about any sexual advantages or transgressions without facing their doom. Vestals even faced punishments for the smallest of errors. Plutarch writes: "If these Vestals commit any minor fault they are punishable by the high-priest only, who scourges the offender."

Christianity and the Emperor Theodosius put an end to the Vestals around 394 AD. The Catholic nun was inspired or recreated from the Vestal Virgin, and they are still tending the sacred secrets. Monasteries have different ways and habits; however, you can find Vesta in every single one. Although times and cultures have changed, much of the idea of the Vestal remains intact.

We can link the Catholic Pope to the Pontifex Maximus, as Pope means "Papa" in Latin. The last major reformation of the Catholic Church began around 1959, ending in change in 1965. Pope John XXIII decided that the Church needed to change with the times on January 25, 1959; this change was called Vatican II or the Second Vatican Council. The Church let go of some overly authoritarian ways and began living more humanely. The Vatican has undergone many changes and continues to reform. Vesta is often present during these transitions; she was opposite the Sun (conjunct the Earth in Leo) during Vatican II, and Pallas was conjunct Juno. On October 11, 1962, with a new Council established reform began. Vesta was conjunct Juno (the Nun standing with the Bride).

Like the first Vestal, many nuns today are still cloistered. (Some traditions never die.) Mild to severe corporal punishment varies as each cloister differs in its ways. Although many progressive nuns of the 1960s gave up their habits for more practical or conservative attire, many younger nuns today embrace the habit.

The dress of the Vestal Virgins made them unique. Later, the Vestals had an elaborate costume that included the *tunica interior* (a simple white chemise worn next to the skin), the *fascia* or *mamillare* (a band of cloth wrapped around the body to hold the breasts in place), the *stola* (a long and covering gown of white trimmed with "purple", e.g. deep red), the *strophia* (a simple tied girdle), and the *palla* (a white cloak, also trimmed with "purple"). They had three "allowed" types of shows, all made of white leather from the skins of sacrificial animals.

Except for the colors, most of the outfit was the same shape of the dress worn by upper-class Roman matrons. (Adulterers and prostitutes were forbidden to wear the stola.) However, their hair was dressed in the *seni crines* a fancy hairstyle with six braids which was only worn by brides. A Vestal's hair was cut off upon initiation and hung on a sacred lotus tree at the temple, and then it was never cut again. The ritual is a symbol of submission, a rite to the goddess. As a Vestal's hair grew longer, it was put it into braids, and as they advanced in stature and age, the number of braids would increase. They wore a *vitta*, a white band that held their hairstyle in place, like many Roman women, but on top of that they wore the *infula*, a white padded woolen band wrapped around the head which was specific to priests. For ceremonial occasions, they wore the *suffibulum*, a short veil of white edged in "purple" and lined with many red and white ribbons, symbolizing the flame of Vesta and their own purity. So their costume was drawn from multiple social classes—they were virgins with the hair of a bride, mothers with the dress of a matron, and a priestly headdress.

Ritual clothing tends to look to the past, and modern Catholic nun's habits are just the ordinary clothing of a married woman in the 11th century, except in special colors—like the costume of the Vestals. Around the 15th century, monks and nuns changed to a darker brown, or black gown/habit. Some nuns are more casual now, but many still wear the typical black habit with which we are most familiar. Even among more casual nuns today, the majority still wear a veil or headdress. Tradition is good to learn, but for Vestals also it is essential to evolve with the times.

The Vestal Virgins were prophetesses and astrologers. Many nuns today are students, teachers, and nurses—both domestic and intellectual. It was said that of the 30-year tenure of a Vestal, the first ten years were spent learning and doing service in the temple, the second ten years were spent doing political and diplomatic work in the outside world, and the third ten years were spent teaching. One could see this as the first ten years of service are feminine/receptive, the next ten years masculine/active, the last ten unified male/female.

How did the Vestal's role change? Laws change all the time; especially when it involves the king. (In early Babylonian times the king might be replaced every time an eclipse would occur. To respect the integrity of the king, the Babylonians studied the eclipse cycle. It is known today as the Saros cycle and is still used to map eclipses.) When a king lacked an heir, the son of a Virgin would become king. Virgin did not always mean a woman with no sexual knowledge; it means a woman who is owned by no man. A woman, such as a priestess, would be known as a virgin and capable of having children.

The Virgin Mary may have been such a woman. The donkey is sacred to the Virgin because it carried her while pregnant. A prophecy, told to king Herod, led to the search and killing of infants who threatened his rulership. It is possible that he would have changed the law regarding priestesses.

The Modern Vestal

Known in ancient Rome as "the salt of the Earth", Vestals provided sustenance. They were the shields of Earth, protecting others from the sufferings of life. The modern healthy Vestal continues to maintain harmony within, despite constant changes in the environment. She does this by having a sacred space, maintaining a healthy environment inside and outside, and embodying integrity and composure in difficult situations. She finds ways to balance and support her nervous system. The modern Vestal can provide a safe place for herself and others, and her fire provides a personal reflection.

Modern Vestals are brave, free, virtuous, and intelligent. In the chart of one of the most well-known nuns, Mother Teresa from Albania, Vesta is in a Taurus Stellium. Mother Teresa was known for her vow of poverty to help the poor. She worked with poor people around the world, including founding her famous hospices in Calcutta, where the local people decided that she was a living embodiment of the goddess Kali.

> *"Let your presence light new light in the hearts of others."* ~Mother Teresa

Chart of Mother Theresa. August 26 1910, 2:25 p.m. Skopie, Macedonia.

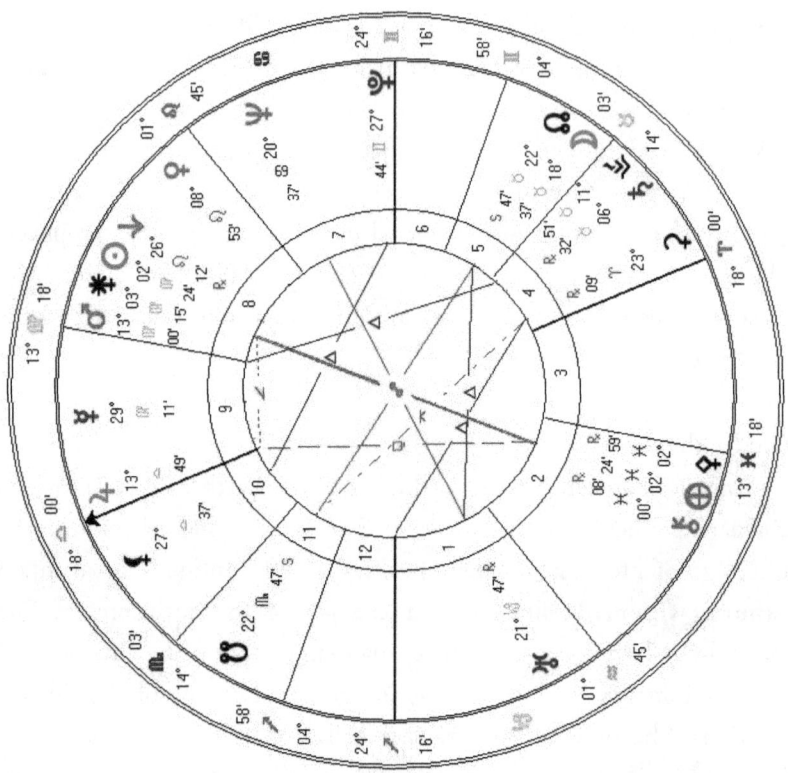

After proper training, a Vestal is a leader of her community. Vestals were and are the peace-makers, silent until they had reason to speak. In Rome, they were part of the state, and their counsel was sought. The Vestals came from no family of political parties; Rome needed to keep that counsel pure and unbiased. Vesta is a diplomat. She is respected, and her word is the word of god/goddess. Hence the reason to speak only gold.

Although others may help along the way, Vestals only have our own experiences. No one can judge what another goes through without experiencing it for themselves. A childless person does not know what it is like to be a parent, a person of one race does not know what it is like to be of another race, and one who has never experienced poverty for themselves does not know what it is like to be poor. To empathize and help others, we need to understand their experiences. Since we never really know what they have experienced unless we experience it for ourselves, it is important for the Vestal to listen to others. The more people one listens to, the more understanding one has about experiences that one can never personally have.

Vestals are the caretakers who do diligent work which generally goes unnoticed by others. Although we may often be taken for granted, we should not be thrown off balance because of this. We must keep our focus and continue our work. We need to be centered in our temples, the temple of the sacred self, the sacred home, and the sacred community/Earth.

In Rome, a Vestal was free from her vows between 36 and 42, depending on when she was initiated. Some Vestals left the temple at that time—retired Vestals were generally prized as wives—and some chose to stay on. Astrologically speaking, this period in life is about the time of the midlife crisis—the Pluto square (depending on what era you were born, as Pluto has an uneven orbit), the Neptune square, and then the Uranus opposition. These transits are followed a few years later by the Saturn opposition at 44 and the Chiron return at 50. In earlier eras with a shorter life span, it was at this time when one would consider entering spiritual life.

> *When Uranus entered Taurus and my 6th house, I became a full-time potter. I took three classes while enrolled in college and later bought a pottery wheel. Now that I have a space for it, I have taken it up once more. I have been making pots ever since. It is a meditation and a spiritual experience. My space in my garden has become a place of bliss. It is there, at my wheel, where I have found stillness, centeredness, and emptiness - the place of Shiva.*

The ancient Vestals attended all festivals, god/goddess rites, and celebrations. They were the purifying factor in the ritual festivities. The focus on Vesta, the sacred flame, is their rite and what we understand as Vestal. "Focus" comes from the Latin word for "hearth", so it is the special study of Vesta. Focus is often a difficult task, especially in the modern world. (Vesta in astrology represents focus and often spiritual desire in positive aspects, and possibly lack of focus and material or mundane desires in the harder aspects.)

Constant focus on the present moment is very Vestal, as is guided meditation and physical yogas/asanas. Any daydreaming can cause you to get burned by the flame. There may have been a good reason behind the ancient Vestal's chastity for 30 years. Loss of focus can lead to problems, as a lack of being continuously present can cause risks to well-being. Love and romance cause a loss of focus. If you have ever been manipulated or blinded by love, then you can understand this analogy.

Whatever gives a Vestal great pleasure in life is a source of energy, as it is our deepest desires which power us forward. There are two types of mundane desires: physical desires and social desires. Physical desires represent our survival, and they may be mostly fulfilled by the self (food, shelter, sex). Social desires represent the survival of society, which is only fulfilled by the group-desire. When used selfishly, any desire can cause an imbalance of the whole and lead to a constant wanting more.

A Vestal seeks to keep society in balance through the fulfillment of desire. She is, in a sense, a martyr. The definition of a martyr is someone who fulfills the desires of others at her own expense. Even though they held themselves away from sexual activity with others, the Roman Vestals were still very much women, and Vesta's asceticism does not negate being female. In fact, men with a strong Vesta in their charts will sometimes be more feminine in their demeanor.

A Vestal must learn presence and self-love. They must learn persistent presence, patience, and self-protection for this reason. By remaining true to themselves and being owned by no one, they can have more emotional and creative space in their lives. They must learn how to balance their emotions with their intellect and their spiritual side.

It is worth it for a Vestal to learn about the occult. It can be useful to learn to align the chakras, as taught in Kabbalah and Eastern metaphysics. One must free oneself from any blocks to practice kundalini rising. I believe that this is another reason Roman Vestals were chosen young--they had not yet lived long enough to develop blockages in their Chakra system. (We'll look at a Vestal approach to chakras in the next chapter.)

To me, all paths lead to the same sacred place. I could not help but incorporate the spiritual teachings I have learned into each other. The more I study, the more spiritual facets of different schools unite or correspond in some way. God and Goddess, no matter their origin, are inherently human. That is, humans made "g-d" in their image as "G-d" made humans in his/hers.

Modern Vestals, of course, learn about sex. Masturbation, sexual preference, sexual diseases, and sexual healing are all areas Vestals might find it worthwhile to study. They can benefit from astrology, science/magic, or Tantra—either the right-handed Tantra (Dakshinachara, focusing on purification) or left-handed Tantra (Vamachara, focusing on transgression of taboo).[3] Neither of those is the "true path"; the whole of it incorporates both sides. BDSM and other psychosexual therapies may be useful to study. All encompass the path of how to develop a sexual relationship not just with others but with one's self.

Bread making and cooking are Vestal arts, as Vesta is a goddess of homemaking, and sexual energy can be channeled into feeding and caring for others. Art is one of the best creative uses of sexual energy. Many artists, even today, go into voluntary celibacy when creative energy is needed for their work. Making pottery, for example, is not just a skill but a meditation. The first step to using a potter's wheel is centering the ball of clay. One must master centering before they can

---

[3] https://nathas.org/en/tradition/tantra/

move on to the next step: opening. When opened, one can begin to pull and shape the clay into the form that is desired.

In many cultures, rituals are used to attach thought-forms to objects. Either they project positive energy into sacred images, or they used them to destroy demons or negativity. The energy becomes infused into a pot or clay figure in the making, and then the pot or figurine is kept in a sacred space or destroyed. Some use a mantra for the ritual. I rarely use mantras. There are many, and they are not unlike magic spells. I prefer to say what I mean. The more specific you are, the better the results of any intention. All words and thoughts are magic spells. Say what you wish, but understand the consequences.

A Vestal Virgin is a vessel. Possessed in and of herself, she is to hold space for those in need. Completely self-owned, she gives what is needed, and then she sets them free. When one seeks to possess a Vestal, the Vestal will feel a strong need to turn away. A Vestal has her ways and her nature; she must be allowed to retreat into herself. If this act becomes thwarted, it can be painful to all involved. Fire and passion burn!

Vestals go through periods where they are turned on or turned off by sacred work. Pure love and the sacredness of the act turns her on. Whatever their sacred work may be, when they can engage with it cleanly and joyfully, it will be healing for them. When work is done unconsciously or perfunctorily, it is not loving and will not bring the healing energy. Self-doubt is a consequence of unconscious living. If one does not feel truly loved, including by oneself, one may busy one's self with unloving tasks. When it is done consciously, it is always an expression of love. This is why Vestals must learn to be with themselves first, to know how to make themselves happy. They need to be one in and of themselves. With self-love mastered, mastering universal love is easier.

The sacredness of love connects us to the cosmos. Universal life energy flows freely, as does conscious love. It is pure, and it is light. There is no end and no beginning. There is only now.

The act of love comes before the physical act of sex. We extend our love into the Universe, and the love returns. The loving light purifies and cleanses in waves of energy. Pulsating and burning, emotional energy clears our inner space, and we enter into a pure state of consciousness.

Pure sexuality is love. A Vestal possesses the love energy of the Earth and serves the evolutionary needs of the Universe. Death is also a process of purification. Breath is a constant exchange, but the removal of oxygen preserves. The energies of life are the essences of the goddess, the embodiment of all that exists, the source of being.

Vesta is the creative motivation that inspires the integration of the whole. She studies the secrets and gives understanding through perception. The unity of self creates solidarity within all that exists. That is the state of being that a Vestal is encouraged to cultivate.

Purity is crucial to all Vestals because the inner consciousness becomes the outer reality. It is imperative that they stay focused on the present because they are powerful beings of creation. Their thoughts can and do become their reality; hence the need to remain present and focused by creating the desired outcome. On some level, Vestals know that what they think becomes their reality. As creators and manifesters, they need to remain present and know what they want.

A Vestal's journey is one of consciousness. They are not just their mind or body. They are mind/body unity to the 12th degree. They reach their highest when love is in balance.

Protection is vital! Vestals need protection. They must be aware of the envy of others and learn to divert the evil eye. They protect themselves through fire and take care of their own needs. The desires of others can test her vows and devotion. But the Vestal has made vows and cannot always provide their desired outcome. How should she handle it? A less experienced or disciplined person would succumb to the desire of the other. At this time, strength comes in handy. They often know when another needs healing; however, disrespect them, their boundaries, or what they consider sacred, and they will cut you off. The best one can do is to honor them for their service, and move forward with life.

Trees find sustenance in the light, and photosynthesis gives the tree energy for the flowers to bloom. The flowers are gifts to the world. They provide beauty and nutrients to fuel the Earth. Vesta in Virgo is represented in assimilation. It is through creation or assimilation that the process begins again. Vesta as the sacred Lotus tree defies gravity (the pull of the material world). Priapus chased Lotis, the nymph, until she turned into a tree of the forest, radiating energy, and hardened herself. Her Vestal energy was so devoted that transformation was the only way. She has no other choice but to accept sex/death/transformation, linking Vesta to Scorpio.

A Vestal has to learn to control her fire. If she is to control her power, she must work on her fire-taming skills. Women are usually taught to be submissive, limited to the role of child-bearers. Vestals must protect their sanctity and sanctuary. Focusing her creativity on the divine pursuits of the goddess, she stands in her power.

Vestals need to take care of themselves first and foremost. I strongly suggest that Vestals should cleanse daily with water—not just for good hygiene, but to absolve all the energies built up. Vestals can take on other energies that are not their own, and running water over their bodies like a ritual is cleansing and purifying. Retreat is also imperative to this ritual; sometimes they must escape from the snares and holds of others.

Jesus was baptized with water to wash away sin, born of a virgin, meant to be king. He initiated others to join him in renunciation. Jesus shared himself with the public, and he often went on retreat to replenish himself after healing and being exposed to others. A martyr, he suffered and sacrificed because of their sins. "But many who are first will be last and the last first." Vesta is the first and the last.

There are many references to the essence of Vesta in the Christian bible; it states that the sacrificial fire came from Yahweh, and that it was to be continually burning. The story of Jesus is very Vestal! The Christian symbol of the fish is a representation of the goddess turned sideways.

Death is a part of the Vestal process. She helps those who are passing over, and she helps those that have already passed over. Like the *bardo* in Buddhism, she guides them through this transition. Ideally, she has the power to save others from death. She may pardon anyone she chooses while maintaining boundaries. Like a snake, a Vestal must shed her skin (attachments, stereotypes, labels, false ego) to grow. She then teaches and heals, allowing others to do the same.

The sacred relationship comes with much refinement and practice. The Vestal must know how to use her Will in all situations to keep herself free from attachments of humanity. She is always to refrain from giving all of herself. When the devotee seeks what she cannot provide and she wants to find a way without compromising herself, this is where her creative determination comes through. Sometimes she will need the help of other Vestals, or she will choose to take the situation onto another path. She may even introduce him/her to their future wife/husband or fate/demise.

A Vestal should be non-judgmental, and should allow space for open at-oneness. People often tell her their secrets. This is because a Vestal's whole vocation is initiation; she ignites the sacred flame in all that seek her. A Vestal knows and understands what people want and desire and what they do not want or desire, and she knows when someone is behaving superficially. Vesta wants no less than the honest self. Sometimes she will dig a little deeper into people to bring out their true selves, or sometimes they offer it to her freely because she provides the space needed to do so.

Although a hermit, a Vestal can be kind, loving, and compassionate. If you are lucky enough to be alone in their presence, you may want to skip the small talk and go straight to your deepest questions/desires. People who come to Vesta need something. Vesta is there to provide them with the spirituality they need. Compassion is boundless; however, boundaries need establishing.

Vestals need to be pure of heart, speaking only what they mean, which requires them to know and trust themselves completely. What they lack is doubt; if they are doubtful, they should not speak. If they say yes, they mean yes, and no means no. Because their word is sacred, their word is respected.

Desires are funny things. Vestals understand desires. They want to advance the race by giving into desires. Some may see desires as a negative thing, but a Vestal knows how important they are to reach our potential and higher spiritual growth. Here is how a desire can play out. Take chocolate cake, for an example. A cake lover wants a piece but decides she had better not. She walks by it, looks at it, and craves it, but she thinks her desire is wrong or evil. She suppresses it. Suddenly she cannot deny herself anymore, and she pinches a small piece to taste. It tastes so good! She eats a little more. "Okay, one piece," she tells herself. But the amount of cake she eats may have less to do with her willpower and more to do with how long she has been denying herself. If she gave in to her desire responsibly, it may have been satiated without much regret. However, if she has too many ambivalent feelings about it, she may end up eating the whole cake and be sick with a stomachache.

When we have a desire, it is better to recognize it and fulfill it in the healthiest way possible. They do not just go away when we refuse them. They will be there building, fermenting, seething until fulfilled. When we fulfill our lowest desires, we can move on to our loftiest ambitions and ascend. Vesta provides the strength needed to overcome.

CHAKRA ASSOCIATIONS

Chakra	Color	Sound	Astrological Association	Sanskrit Name
Earthstar	Black	AUM	Pluto and Ceres	Vasundhara "wealth" or "earth"
Root	Red	LAM	Saturn, Capricorn and Aquarius	Muladhara "root"
Sacral	Orange	VAM	Jupiter, Sagittarius, and Pisces	Svadisthana "self-established"
Solar Plexus	Yellow	RAM	Mars, Aries, and Scorpio	Manipura "lustrous gem"
Heart	Green	YAM	Venus, Taurus and Libra	Anahata "unstruck"
Throat	Blue	HAM	Mercury, Gemini, and Virgo	Vishuddhi "purest"
Third Eye	Indigo/Violet	OM	Sun, Moon, Cancer, Leo	Ajna "perceive" or "command"
Crown	Purple	AUM	The Cosmos	Sahasrara "thousand-petaled"
Soul Star	Magenta	silence	Beyond the Universe	Padaka "footprint" or "foundation"

A Vestal Look at the Chakras

As I've said before, everything I study tends to get integrated into one whole body of knowledge. There is a lot to be said for working with Chakras. You can refer to the chart for their colors, sounds, and other associations. Before working with any of the upper Chakras, always begin with the root or Earthstar. A good meditation is to concentrate on each of the Chakras. Begin by feeling the Earth hold you (Earth Chakra). After feeling "grounded" (held by the Earth), open by chanting OM or AUM.

Move on to the next Chakra, the Root. Chant LAM, with your hands near the root. There are mudras (hand gestures) for each chakra, which are easy to find online with a web search. You can use the mudra for each chakra, or place the hands over the chakra being worked. The Root color is red; hold that color in the minds-eye while chanting LAM.

After you feel that it is open (a couple of seconds to minutes), move up your body and focus on the sacral chakra. Focus on orange; chant VAM. Move up the body, putting focus on each chakra. Take as much time as needed. Some chakras may need more time to open than others. Once the root is open, you can work on the individual chakras. I suggest always doing them in order and then spend more time with the ones that need the most work.

- ❖ Earthstar Chakra: Earth under our feet, connects with center. When blocked: Feeling disconnected to the Earth. Ungrounded, destructive to Mother Nature, or the self. Sound: When open, we ground to the Earth. With Earth's vibrations felt, she speaks to us through words, unspoken. We feel the need to protect her. She is our connection to the core of Gaia. The Earth Chakra's essence is the Goddess Pachamama or Inanna, Goddesses of the fertile Earth and underworld.
- ❖ Root Chakra: When blocked: Feelings of uncleanliness, unsafe, or hunger. Body shame. Sadness or fear of being alone. When open, we are rooted and secure. When we connect with the Earth, she

holds us. We have child-like receptivity. Our spine straightens, and we are aware of ourselves. We have everything we need. The Root Chakra's essence is the Hindu God, Ganesha, Remover of Obstacles.

- Sacral Chakra: When blocked: Sexual inhibitions or issues from sexual abuse, self-consciousness, sore muscles, digestive problems, shame, guilt, or anger toward the opposite sex. When open, self-assured, happy being who we are in our place and space. Being able to express how we feel freely and openly. The spot where we feel the vibration from the physical connection. The Sacral Chakra's essence is the Hindu Goddess, Shakti, Goddess of Power.
- Solar Plexus Chakra: The Powerhouse. When blocked: Low self-esteem. Dissatisfaction. Food sensitivities, fatigue, lack of drive, uncertainty. When open, we are strong and confident. By owning a powerful Will, we can store energy. Satisfaction comes from helping others. The Solar Plexus Chakra's essence is the Hindu God, Agni, God of Fire.
- Heart Chakra: Love and Serenity. When blocked: Repression of Love. Disease of the heart. Repression of self, nature, or the cosmos. Disrupted sleeping patterns, desperation, desire to end life, sadness, grief, or heartache. Becoming open to love, to touch, to heal, unattached, unhurt, unbeaten. Acceptance. Faith and faithfulness. The Heart Chakra's essence is the Hindu God, Vishnu, God of Preservation. "Green frees sensuality and allows the body to guide the spirit before the mind can guide the body." -Laura Tuan
- Throat Chakra: Thyroid/Pure Voice. When blocked: Repression of speech. Lies and deception. Stiffness in neck, shoulders, or throat. Confusion, repressed emotions. Forced to be silent. Open to sing, communicate through vibration, expressing your truth and at-oneness. All paths lead to the same "Supreme Consciousness". The Throat Chakra's essence is the Hindu God, Shiva, God of Dissolution.

- Third Eye Chakra: Brow/Nervous system/Clairvoyance/Intuition. When blocked: Trouble sleeping, or concentrating, headaches, anxiety, holding a grudge, repression of imagination, fear of rejection, lack of Vision, illusions or hallucinations. When open, clear intuition through visions and dreams. Mental clarity through meditation. Kundalini energy can rise from the Agnya (third eye) to the Sahasrara (crown) for the highly developed. The Third Eye Chakra's essence is the Hindu Goddess, Apas, Goddess of Water.
- Crown Chakra: The Divine Union, higher self. When blocked: Depression, hypertension, repressing your first inclinations, fear of being alone, fear of the past, guilt or feeling abandoned by the holy. When open, thoughtless enlightenment. Knowing the higher self, universal consciousness, higher awareness. Contact with the father/mother. The Divine Consciousness. Centeredness around the central channel. More energy to focus and concentrate on the commitment of spiritual work. The Crown Chakra's essence is all of the Hindu Gods.
- Soul Star Chakra: Connection to Universal Consciousness. When blocked: Feelings of not belonging. Sound: Silence. When open: Bliss. Complete relaxation and oneness. Love from the highest vibration where the energy of love flows. The Godhead.

Aum, Lam, Vam, Ram, Yam, Ham, Om, Aum... silent.

A Connection to Kabbalah

As kundalini rises, the Root Chakra unites with the Crown Chakra. It is an ascension of Jacob's ladder. Our spiritual energy can extend as much as seven feet past our bodies. When kundalini rises, the tree of life does as well. Malchut becomes Kether, the Godhead, and Kether, the godhead transcends. Malchut is also recognized as Shekhinah/Shakti/Spirit and rises to a higher level. The path to ascension is as difficult as it seems.

Malchut is the Earth, the root, and earthly things; Keter is the crown and the godhead. Sex and earthly things become spiritualized

Shekhinah is the feminine, the goddess of the Hebrews; similar to Shakti, the feminine aspect and goddess of Hinduism, or Sophia the Holy Spirit in Christianity—the concept is the same. In Kabbalah, the Sephirot are parts of the human condition. Binah is said to be the Superior Mother, Malchut is the Inferior Mother. As above, so below. The goddess encompasses all. She is both superior and inferior, and all that besets in-between.

Binah, in Kabbalah, is the fire connected with Vesta (also Saturn). Binah is the sacred fire and the Earth. The fire of Binah is concealed so that all that lie within are transmuted or transformed. The process is similar to alchemy or the hardening of greenware in the potter's kiln.

Vesta and the Other Goddesses

> *"International cooperation has been necessary for both the observation of asteroids and computation of their orbits."* -Encyclopedia Americana

Vesta orbits the Sun, but all of the goddess asteroids lean toward Jupiter. Their orbits flow in relationship to each other. They work together to form the largest part of the asteroid belt, known as the goddess asteroids. The world came together to communicate information about the asteroids and their astrological meanings for the best understanding of them. Together, these goddesses represent global cooperation. When we use asteroids in astrology, we are using global cooperation. We are all connected to one body, the Earth, and her relatives near and far. Goddess asteroids are an integral part of coming together as a whole.

In mythology, Juno is Jupiter's wife, Pallas is his daughter, Ceres and Vesta are his sisters, and Hygeia is his great-granddaughter. Ceres, Pallas, and Vesta are the three largest goddess asteroids. Many cults and religions have the mention of the Three. There is the trinity of a body, mind, and spirit; the father, the son, and the holy spirit; the mother, the maiden, the crone: biology, psychology, ecology, etc. Whether it is the Christian Trinity, the Dianic Trinity, the Hindu Trimurti, the three Fates, or another three, they all represent the birth, preservation, and destruction. Love, Law, and Will. Hence the mention of other goddesses. Although they are all connected, they represent different, independent forms. Like independent countries brought together for a higher cause, the goddess planets work together to shape the whole and require that we do the work together.

The issue here is that these asteroids should not be seen as entirely separate entities. It creates holes in our understanding when they become separated and segmented.

Vesta is the goddess of priests and priestesses. In the Vesta cult, all rites to the gods/goddesses begin and end with Vesta. However, part of

Vestal training is learning about other gods/goddesses (or other aspects of the self).

Gods and goddesses do not usually derive from a place of historically reasonable origin. Vesta was a Roman goddess, and her Greek equivalent is Hestia, but Hestia has equivalents in other cultures such as the Hindu goddess Durga. It amazes me when I study different pantheons of goddesses and find how similar they are. Ancient goddesses have been anglicized or demonized by modern Abrahamic religion, and some have essentially anglicized some aspects while demonizing others.

The Hindu goddess Durga, also represented as one of many different aspects of Kali (or vice versa), is similar to Vesta. Durga is a virgin goddess, owned by no man but summoned by the gods to do battle. She is a beautiful warrior goddess, not unlike Pallas Athene that sprang from the head of a god. The name Durga means "beyond reach" or "impassable" or "unassailable", which is also how the Greeks and Romans describe all their virgin goddesses.

Ceres

Ceres, the nurturing/smothering/sanitizing mother. Ceres loves unconditionally. When love takes leave, she brings death. She controls the seasons. Ceres is also known for milk and blood flow, blood rituals, and rites of womanhood. Ceres represents the child's transition into womanhood through menstruation, childbirth, and the mother. Before people sacrificed animals for ritual use, they valued the menstrual blood; it is still worshiped today as a rite of passage.

Ceres knows intuitively when her children need her. At her best, she knows instinctively what her child needs. She is the wolf-mother, possibly representing Lupercalia, the feminine wolf that nursed the founders of Rome. Romulus and Remus were under the protection of this goddess.

Ceres and Vesta both find purpose in grain and foodstuffs. Ceres is involved with crop and weather manipulation; she grows the food, and then it is turned over to Vesta to count and distribute. Vesta counts on a good harvest to preserve, and she provides for the larger community.

Ceres is the bringer and destroyer of the seasons. Vesta is the bringer of evolution. If biology has anything to do with it, statistically, women hit puberty before men, and they have many seasons.

Figure 4: *Goddess Dhumavati "The Smoky One" on Crow/Goose Chariot, A Group Of Four Illustrations Of Devis. Circa 1830. Mandi, India.*

Ceres can represent the mother, the maiden, or the crone. I see her Crone form as being like Dhumavati ("she who is made of smoke"), and crows or other blackbirds are her totem. She takes things as they come. Dhumavati is one of the many goddess-forms of Shakti, or one part of the spectrum of spirituality in Tantra. Dhumavati is the ugly old hag with a bowl of fire in one hand and a winnowing basket in the other. She is old age and represents letting go before death. Often it is only during old age when a mother can escape from her mundane life to concentrate on her spiritual life. Dhumavati has let go of so much, but she must continue her journey of detachment and renunciation through teaching and caring for the young. She brings sickness and death; people worship her to keep these things at bay.

The Germanic goddess Holda is a bridge between the nature of Ceres and of Vesta; she is both mother goddess and unmarried crone. Holda, like Vesta, is a household goddess, and cooking, cleaning, and spinning are her sacred holy rites. Her dark nature is the taker of dead infants. She is the darkness of the Yuletide.

Pallas

Vesta is also connected to Pallas. Pallas, linked to the serpent and the owl, waits patiently for advancement. Vesta works diligently to achieve that advancement. She uses Pallas's warrior/masculine energy to push her. When centered within herself, s/he can create without another. S/he needs no other.

The masculine force. The outspoken, creative warrior. Pallas, an androgynous virgin, is the more active aspect of the feminine. She chooses an active or permeative role in military and government operations as opposed to domestic life. The artist, the creative power, masculine and feminine, Pallas is the social justice warrior and suggests gender and role change. People with strong Pallas aspects can be creative artists, or they may be androgynous or transgendered. They are often playfully in touch with both their feminine and masculine sides, regardless of what physical gender they may be.

Pallas is also known to invoke kundalini energy as the connecter of the male/female energies. She has the deep urge to create, linking her to the fifth house in astrology. Pallas represents the scribe as opposed to the housekeeper. She is wise and educated but may lack finesse in feminine ways.

Vesta is stern and knows herself; Pallas throws themself passionately into work. Vesta is the devoted housewife or servant of her community, and Pallas is involved with war games, strategy, patterns, and business. Vesta is the cook, and Pallas works out of the home. Vesta is the ability to focus, and Pallas is the ability to see patterns in information and situations. Vesta is on the right, and Pallas is on the left. Both are needed for balance.

Metis, the wife of Zeus/moon of Jupiter, is her mother, and Vesta, her aunt. Metis was swallowed up by Zeus while pregnant. Their daughter, Athene, was born from his head, a Daddy's Girl, but equal to her father in strength and wisdom. (Her androgyny is such that she can make a man give birth.) With God as her father she can have a swelled head or be very egotistical.

As the serpent goddess, she has roots in many ancient religions. Snakes and serpents are references to wisdom and prophecy. They are linked with goddesses all around the world. The kundalini energy, known as coiled around and at the base of the spine, is represented as a serpent. Ancient artifacts and Isis-Hathor-Sekhmet reveal a headband with a serpent rising from the forehead representing "the Eye of Wisdom". When the kundalini energy rises and escapes through the crown or the head, one has gained wisdom from the goddess. Ishtar and Inanna are also known snake goddesses. The serpent equals wisdom and regeneration.

The Pythia of Delphi was a prophetess who provided divine revelations through oracles, and snakes were sacred inhabitants of the oracular shrine at Delphi. She had a pet snake, Python. Python was a female; although, that thought later changed and Python became known as male. (Pythons have a life span of around 30 years, by the way.) Pythia, or the Oracle, sat upon a tripod over a crevasse, which released noxious vapors. The gases escaping from the Earth are toxic, volcanic fumes; possibly methane, ethane, and ethylene. She was then said to have visions or prophecies of the future. Some got sick or went mad, and some died.

Figure 5: *Pythia on the Tripod. As High Priestess of the Temple of Apollo at Delphi, she served as the Oracle of Delphi. Wood engraving after a drawing by Heinrich Leutemann (German painter, 1824 – 1905), published in 1880. The Temple of Apollo/Delphi is a World Heritage Site.*

Many goddess temples were seized by male dominance and changed to a Temple of God, such as Zeus or Apollo, the Gods who wrestled with Python. The priestesses still held some power in the temples, however, and were revered for holy devotion and respected counsel.

Pallas understands kundalini through the serpent. She is present in all birth charts and likely prominent in kundalini charts, but she is not the driving force behind it. In alchemy, you need an activator and an inhibitor. Uranus and Vesta together are the activator and the inhibitor—the light penetrating the vessel.

Like Vesta, Pallas needs a great work in which to sink their energy. Pallas, imbued with feminine and masculine energies, must have many outlets to satiate them. Art is a go-to. Both Vesta and Pallas use art for meditative practice. Pallas is the patron of the craftsman. She is the genius and inspiration behind the hero. She desires physical activity, and her sexual prowess *requires* physical activity, whereas Vesta is the bread maker, the potter, and the creative hearth.

Creativity is what turns on Pallas. She loves the artist and the creative genius. Kundalini rising is often a breakthrough in inhibitions. The Goddess awakens passion and she feels the vibration in all living things. When in perfect balance, Pallas can go into battle blindfolded and come out victorious. She is delicately aware of her environment and can be hypersensitive and responsive. Wise as the serpent, her bite is far the worst. Pallas loves men, but if they piss her off, she will not work with them or will end their career possibly by doing it herself. The Goddess of wisdom and all trades feels the need to compete. She learns all in preparation for that competition, usually turning her competitor into her friend or vice versa; especially, if he/she is a part of her.

Pallas inspires men and women. She is the hero that resides within. Her spiritual and creative ecstasy will lead to wholeness of self. Attuned to the natural rhythms of the Earth, she links the Root Chakra to the Crown Chakra. She seeks out sexual healing to align the two. Likened to Mercury, Pallas flies freely and accesses her information at will. The Olive tree belongs to Pallas.

Inner knowledge, patience, growth, fertility, sex, art, and hard work guide us through obstacles and opportunities. Counsel, strategy, and diplomacy are the natural response of Pallas. Honor has no fear, and love has no vengeance.

Hygeia

Hygeia is the goddess of hygiene and prevention medicine; her name means wholeness, health, and Earth. Self-care is sacred to her. An herbalist, she harvests Self-Heal during the full moon and preserves medicinal plants for winter. Hygeia is about maintaining overall good health and fitness through mind, body, and sound. She uses herbs to keep the immune system strong.

Hygeia was one of the goddesses invoked in the original Hippocratic Oath.[4] Her father is the healer, Asclepius, and their symbols are well known in the pharmacy profession. A human portrayal of Hygeia is a young woman with a pet snake wrapped around her body, drinking from her chalice.

Society has placed more concern on marriage and business contracts (Juno) than they have on self-care and hygiene (Hygeia). But when we discuss the goddess, self-care *is* paramount. After all, Hygeia ranks number four among the largest asteroids, or three if considering Ceres as the dwarf planet. Hygeia, though one of the largest, is one of the dimmest asteroids from Earth's perspective. Planets with the most mass often have more influence over us, however. We feel her more than we see her. The asteroid number for Hygeia is 10.

Hygeia is the clean one, or the one that attends to herself, or preps for an operation. She is feminine cleanliness. Ceres, Pallas, Vesta—the triple goddess + Hygeia. When one empowers these four goddesses, she is complete in her feminine power.

Juno

Skipping Hygeia and going to Juno in astrology seems to hold marriage as a higher standard than self-care. Perhaps a progression from religion to enlightenment will see that it has flipped. I was surprised to learn that the four largest asteroids are Ceres, Vesta, Pallas, and Hygeia. I was expecting Juno because those are the four main asteroid goddesses most mentioned in astrology (Ceres, Vesta, Pallas, Juno). Juno was the 4th discovered, and is the 11th largest asteroid in the asteroid belt.

Juno represents commitments, contracts, wealth, and admiration. In mythology, it appears she has an intense relationship with her husband, Zeus/Jupiter. Juno is married to God. She is Hera, the queen of heaven, and her position is her power. She does not want to give up

---

❖ [4] https://doctors.practo.com/the-hippocratic-oath-the-original- and-revised-version/#The_Classic_Hippocratic_Oath

her seat; she wants what is hers. As queen of Heaven, Juno can have her way and get it in writing.

Juno may represent past-life/karmic ties in synastry. Although she rules the marriage contract, Vesta rules the changing of family. Juno is the legal licensing, and Vesta is the ritual bonding.

Kali

Now I am moving from the Greek to the Hindu goddesses. First is Kali, the powerful goddess of wisdom, the awakener. Kali is protection, destruction, and creation. She represents time, the beginning, the passing, the end. Kali as destruction, or the cremation ground, represents the processes and cycle of death. Kali can be likened to Lilith as she is the devouring mother. The downward-pointing triangle, her *yoni*, is where the dead rest and are reborn. It is universal creativity, a black hole, where the dead are burnt up and resurrected, the sacred womb of creation. Kali is the pulse of the heart; she is "Mother Time". There are twelve Kalis and twelve zodiac signs. As a Scorpio, the Firebird would say "A little self-destruction does wonders for growth."

Vesta has a dark side, if you believe in duality. She is focused, but she is just as likely to be unfocused. She is devotional, or she can lack devotion. Fire concentrated, cultivated, and watched over, hurts no one, but the fire left to its own devices burns all in its path.

> *"We have suffered the consequences of unbalanced power for long enough. Our world cannot any longer tolerate the disruption and destruction brought about by demonic force. In the present ... Kali is the answer, and she will have to annihilate again to reveal the truth of things, which is her mission, and to restore to our natures that divine feminine spirituality which we have lost"* ~A. Mookerjee.

Shakti

Vesta shows herself in the goddess Shakti, the energy and cause of kundalini rising. She reveals true consciousness and a state of bliss. The

Divine Mother Herself is everything! She is all that is, was, and all that ever will be because she creates it. Shiva is eternal emptiness, space, and sometimes the lack that needs fulfilling. He is our peace and our stillness. When Shakti surrenders unto Shiva, they are one in eternal bliss. A give and take of divine energy, creating, holding, and releasing.

Shakti is the "Shining One", the feminine force and the life-giving energy of the universe, with many names and faces. By performing Puja to Shakti, the devotee attains what they desired. Shakti delivers us from suffering. She is the bringer of bliss.

For those who have fulfilled their material desires or those who believe that they must not have material things, what would they wish to attain from a Shakti Puja? Shakti opens our hearts to absolute love, absolute freedom & absolute wholeness. To reach the highest consciousness, we must practice love. We cannot think about spirituality; we have to live it! Discipline and devotion are required.

The Puja can be done much the same for solitary practitioners.[5] Cultivating a sensitivity to Shakti through practice allows an ease of her energy to flow through you. This blissful experience affects the whole being. Kundalini rising, the Shakti energy that flows freely through the chakra system, is often felt as ripples in time and space, vibrating, circling, or a full-body orgasmic state. Practice makes it sufficient and sparky, and one may even cultivate it at will. Other awakeners can transmit this energy to you. The connection is between souls.

Shekhinah (Holy Spirit) is the Hebrew or Jewish equivalent of Shakti. Others may recognize her as Sofia. Shekhinah or Shakti is known as the dwelling place of God or Shiva. It is the reasoning behind the god and the goddess being one of the same; just as the body cannot live without the spirit from above, the ghost cannot live without a body. Binah, in the Kabbalistic tree, may relate to Shakti and its opposite Chokhmah to Shiva. The tree of life can also represent the body. When Binah and Chokhmah rise together, they become Keter, divine love.

---

[5] https://www.shaktisadhana.50megs.com

Shakti separated herself from Shiva and became innumerable goddesses. She, in her different forms, would again marry Shiva to be united once more. It is on the plane of duality that they separate; when creativity manifests. But knowing that they are not separate and treating each as an aspect of self, they can unite again by throwing off the delusion of duality.

Shakti creates, from herself, the male form; therefore, she can manifest from herself alone. Shakti is the first energy created. She is eternal and limitless. In her light form, she is Gauri, the virgin lover. In her dark form, she is Kali, the demon destroyer. Shakti is the creator of the elements, and therefore the controller and disintegrator of them.

The path of God/Shiva is devotion, knowledge, and love. Shiva is the space that holds us. Shakti is the light or energy that fills the emptiness. Shiva and Shakti can create from nothingness or destroy all that is. Vesta, or a Vestal, emulates Shakti.

Like the triple goddess, there are three Shaktis in the Tantra Yoga tradition. There are as many yogas as there are lifestyles—perhaps too many to summarize in one book. In Kriya Tantra Yoga, the three forms of Shakti are Iccha, Jňana, and Kriya. Iccha Shakti is the energy of will, desire, and intention. Jňana Shakti is the energy of knowledge, the mind, thoughts, and intuition. Kriya Shakti is the action, manifestation, and results. We are in constant flux; when one of the energies is not in use, there is often stagnation.

New Age yogis suggest a fourth, Shakti—the Kundalini-Shakti. Like yoga, the kundalini craze has given new names to old traditions. The original yoga to raise Kundalini, for example, is Hatha Yoga. It focuses on the breath and movement of the body. Yoga Basics (www.yogabasics.com) uses this fourth Shakti to describe Kundalini rising, a typical result of the first three. If that is the will, we gain the knowledge, and the action activates the inner channel of energy that flows through the whole chakra system. The Shakti energy from the root rises to electrify and awaken our senses. It is like we are plugging into the Earth. The body connects to the mind. The heart is the bridge. The path is open; the root connects to the crown.

Hadit

Hadit is the Thelema Sky Goddess, derived from the Egyptian sky goddess Nut or Nuit, whom I also see as connected to Vesta. Hadit connects us to the heart chakra (Anahata) and the Star of David. Hadit is the upward-pointing triangle, and Nuit is the downward-pointing triangle. This union creates an explosive awakening, pain or bliss, as if to suggest a Kundalini rise.

Aleister Crowley, the founder of Thelema, describes Hadit/Nuit as a lover. She is the night sky, naked and shining with stars. She could be seen as a Tantra goddess, the way Crowley explains her: "I give unimaginable joys on earth..."

This goddess meets in the present and has certainty in life and death. Free from fear, she is the peace and ecstasy in the mind/body. Through raising Kundalini energy, she can transform at will. She lives life to the fullest and accepts death as it comes. Hadit and her followers each experience life as it is happening, including death. Death is just one of many life transitions.

Lilith

Of course, I cannot discuss goddesses without mentioning the infamous Lilith! There are multiple astrological Liliths. Black Moon Lilith (true or mean), the central astronomical point of the moon's orbit (the lunar apogee, or the point farthest from Earth), is the main one most used in astrology. The asteroid Lilith(1181) is in the asteroid belt with the other goddess planets. The star Algol is the star of Lilith according to the ancient Hebrews. There are a couple more even less known Liliths, but that is another book entirely.

Lilith was a goddess of the desert and a goddess of lust and barrenness. Sent by the goddess Ishtar/Inanna to lead men astray, Lilith performed sexual rites with them in her temple to honor her mistress. She originally lived in a huluppu tree with a serpent at the bottom and a bird at the top, which is reminiscent of Kundalini.

In Kabbalah, Lilith may represent Malchut or the lower Shekhinah or goddess energy. Vesta would be the upper Shekhinah in the Tree of Life. By joining the two, they become one. Lilith is the tree roots hiding in the earth, and Vesta is the crown and branches extending toward the heavens. Lilith is the forest floor, and Vesta is the canopy, similar to the lower chakra (root) joining with the upper chakra (crown).

In ancient cultures, she is a temple priestess of the goddess. In patriarchal religions, such as Hebrew, she is born from the moon after G-d diminished her (lunar) light. Although born equal to Adam as his first wife, she was enraged at the thought of lying beneath him (missionary position only). By uttering the secret name of G-d, she sprouted wings and disappeared from Eden and Adam. The story goes on to tell how she found exile near the Red Sea where she copulated with demons and spawned thousands of sex-demon children who G-d would try to destroy.

I have heard that Black Moon Lilith is associated with truth. True spirituality is truth, so Lilith is related in that she is the foundation of spiritual truth. We rebel so that we can learn for ourselves. The truth is not always pretty; however, it is erotic. The endorphins released during sexual climax are the same as those released during spiritual climax. To some, there is no difference.

Lilith represents both unbridled sexuality and the destruction of the sexually created (abortions, dead babies, destruction of man, etc.) and Vesta represents repressed sexuality that gives birth to man/god/sons of G-d. Through her controlled sexuality she creates and sustains man/god/herself. Either way, the goddess is recognized by her sexuality and her procreative power. Vesta takes on the responsibilities and commitment of sex and sexual energy. She is the unification of sex and represents conscious sexuality. In a sense, Vesta is Lilith spiritualized.

In astrology, Lilith's placement is connected to the moon. We are not, per se, our Sun sign. We are born at a specific time during the moon. The zodiac sign and phase of the moon are major astrological and feminine contributors to our natal charts. Black Moon Lilith represents the center of the moon's ecliptic around the Earth. Lilith centers the moon. Since the moon orbits the Earth, and is, therefore, a part of the Earth, her influence is subtle or subconscious.

Lilith has needs, and Vesta has fulfilled those needs. Vesta provides the space, the warmth, and the sustenance. Lilith is pure sexual desire, the hidden behind the motivation, the exiled in the muddy emotions, our shadow. Vesta accepts her.

Vesta requires limitations; Lilith breaks limitations. Lilith can be hysterical when sexual enjoyment becomes suppressed. When she begins the illumination process by going inward (Vesta), those dirty emotions from religious dogma may creep up for examination. It is imperative to examine and re-examine beliefs as they often change with experience. In this case, Lilith is the truth. She appears when our energies are blocked. Lilith may help to release any strongholds on our nature. She is the self we cannot deny.

Brigid

The perpetual flame of St Brigit in Kildare, Ireland, still burns today![6] Brigit or Brigid is a sacred Irish deity that became Christianized around the fifth century when travelers brought their own beliefs to Ireland. Brigid, like Vesta, was a Pagan goddess and both were worshipped with ritual fires. Prayers to the goddess are often to protect the meek and domesticated animals and for a fruitful harvest.

Brid is the triple goddess. Dagda (the father-god) had three daughters who all made up one goddess; one was associated with poetry (Vesta), one with smithcraft (Pallas), and the third with healing

---

[6] http://kildare.ie/heritage/details.asp?GCID=140
http://kildarelocalhistory.ie/kildare/history-of-kildare-town/saint-brigid/2/
https://ucdculturalheritagecollections.com/2018/01/25/st-bridgit-of-kildare-patron-of-the-powerless/

(Ceres). Brigid is kind and cares for those who are destitute. Her flame shines bright and is ever-burning through an endless supply of the holy spirit. She has many names, including Brid, Brigantia, and Brigit. Known as "the poetess", Brid territory is water, and rivers carry her name. She is a household deity and serves everyday ordinary people. Through the people and their reliance on livestock, healing, and the fruit-of-the-earth, she survived Pagan banning and became a Christian saint. Allowed to keep their position in literary/historical/legal responsibilities and document keeping, the priestesses of Brid were nearly removed from their role in ritual worship when Christianity moved in. One woman, however, "accidentally" became ordained as a bishop.

This world-renowned saint is known as St. Brigid, or Mary of the Gael. She was considered the embodiment of the goddess of Ireland. Witty and compassionate, she freed prisoners, slaves (including her mother), and protected anyone that came through her door/fire, including wanted criminals. Her power was immense, and she was revered by the kings, magnates, and noblemen she constantly outsmarted.

The story of St. Brigid and the nuns/priestess of the Perpetual Flame is quite remarkable in its similarities to Vesta and the Roman Vestal Virgins. St. Brigid was born in 453 A.D; her father was a nobleman and her mother a slave. She was sold and brought up in a Druidic household. Rumor says St. Brigid converted her Druidic family to Christianity. After many adventures, St. Brigid was no stranger to battle, and settled in her hometown. She chose to build her oratory on a hillside under a sacred oak. Oak leaves are both symbolizes of Druidism and Christianity, as well as Kildare.

St. Brigid's dedication to keeping the fire lit became tradition. Together with nineteen others, St. Brigid took her part in sustaining the fire. Each night one would be responsible for tending the flame, and on the 20th night, St. Brigid took that station. It is the custom for the priestesses of the Perpetual Flame at Kildare. Brigid is celebrated around the world today on Imbolc/Candlemas (Feb 1). It is the day the

Sun returns to the Northern Hemisphere and the divine spark of creativity emerges from the fire of the virgin goddess.

Renuka/Yellamma[7]

The cult of Yellamma has many similarities to the cult of Vesta. Yellamma, one of many forms of the goddess and consort of Shiva, is a household deity found throughout India. Her worship is predominantly among the lower caste system. The belief or system behind this culture is duality. Yellamma relates to color/darkness, cold/heat, sickness/health, and sexuality/disgust; these find use in her rituals. This goddess represents women in their most erotic state; Yellamma is male/female; erotic/ascetic, a worker in a spiritual sense. Sex is fun and natural. It makes us happy when done correctly. Devadasi (initiates of the goddess) are artisans, entertainers, and ritual organizers. Through the joy and power of creation, expressing our femininity connects us to the divine.

Yellamma is the "divine mistress". This goddess is portrayed as the aroused one. Her powerfully sexual feminine heat provides the arena for transformation, which can show itself in many forms and oppositions. Male-to-female and female-to-male transformations occur with this goddess. The women may take on a more masculine approach in action and earning a living, not typical in patriarchal societies. The men portraying the goddess are called *jogappa*, and the women depicting ascetic life are called *jogamma*. They are "caught" by Yellamma and are her human servants from whom she works.

Many gods/goddesses of the Hindu pantheon are of both genders, or they may incarnate sometimes as a man and sometimes as a woman. Yellamma is the goddess of transgenderism, and thus is linked to the Greek Pallas. She accepts that men can be feminine and erotic, and women can be masculine, active, or spiritually ascetic. Initiates, the

---

[7] Bradford, N. (1983). Transgenderism and the Cult of Yellamma: Heat, Sex, and Sickness in South Indian Ritual. *Journal of Anthropological Research, 39*(3), 307-322. Retrieved December 2, 2020, from http://www.jstor.org/stable/3629673

Devadasi, traditionally take up their duties either ritually or non-ritually. Temple dancers are the most prestigious, and therefore, typically of higher caste. Some helped the dancers in performances, celebrations, and rituals, and others took part in helping with their dress and adornments, garlands and flowers. The high priestess, or most talented and beautiful, are titled *Nagarvadhu*, "The Bride of the City".

The spiritualization of transgender is auspicious. The integration of the masculine and the feminine is one of the highest spiritual attainments. Feminine men are considered the "carriers of Yellamma". It is through times of transition when the initiate calls upon the goddess. The *jogappa* (the male Devadasi) has transformed into the goddess. They change their appearance to represent Yellamma after reaching maturity. For some, becoming a devadasi allowed the avoidance of marriage. When a jogappa (male-to-female transgender person) transitions, their dress changes to the dress of the Devadasi. A red sari, typical of bridal attire, is adorned. They are given a feminine name and tattooed. Many may wear their hair in a jedi (a long matted braid) or up in a bun. A Devadasi, female or transgender, can be spotted by their red and white beaded necklace, given at initiation.

The ancients (and some modern worshipers) see the devadasis as the goddess incarnate herself. Highly respected for their access to divine power, they are known to dance until they drop. Many may dance by themselves in a trance and sometimes invoking the goddess into them. Devadasi, maybe dually compensated for their art.

Devadasi means "Goddess servant", God's slave girl, or servant of Shiva. Devadasi initiated as young as six years. A ritual marriage to the divine took place before they entered the temple. In more modern times, Devadasis marry Yellamma's (Renuka's) husband, Jamadagni, the father of Parashuram.

Renuka's story is thus: Yellamma/Renuka was a princess and a devotee of Shiva. She found herself attracted to Jamadagni, an ascetic devotee of Shiva, and proposed to him even though their castes were clearly different. Jamadagni gave her the task of collecting water from the river. She was to make a vessel from the sand of the river bank to carry water back to him. She did so, and he accepted her into his ashram. One day, while collecting water, Renuka saw a man and his bride playing joyfully in the river. She wished that her husband and herself would play like that. She had an impure thought. Her vessel made from sand fell apart, so that she was no longer able to carry water. She returned home empty-handed and Jamadagni sent her away.

After some time in the forest, she came back to the ashram with matted hair and diseased. Jamadagni ordered their three sons to kill her. Parashuram, the eldest son, was said to be with Shiva. When he returned, Jamadagni ordered him to kill Renuka. Parashuram obeyed his father and removed her head with an ax. Jamadagni rewarded his son by granting his desires. Parashuram wished for his mother to come back to life, and Kali, or the demon that possessed his father, to be sent away. At some point, another maiden had interfered in the beheading. Her head was placed on Renuka's, and Renuka's head placed upon the maiden's body. With Ganesha's blessing or by human error Renuka now had the body of the maid and the head of a princess.

This story, like many myths or legends, has some variations. Other philosophies or cultures have had their influence. Some of the oldest traditions come from South India, where tree worship and Tantric religions originated. In the Tantric tradition every individual being is respected and honored as who they are.

Devadasi are the equivalent of the Vestal or other temple priestess. They were worshipped as the goddess and given a piece of government land to cultivate. The school of thought and the way of living for the Devadasi has changed quite dramatically. In the beginning, they were the dancers at the temple rituals. Honored and treated with respect, they took charge of the ceremonies. They were entertainers summoned by Shiva, and could do whatever they wanted. The ancient Devadasis performed many acts, including beautifying the temples. They were the directors of the musical arts, parades, feasts, and funeral processions. The most talented, were celebrated. Marriage was neither forced nor forbidden.

The locals of Saundatti, near the temple, worship Renuka/Yellamma as she gives them happiness. People go to her temple and pray to the goddess and it is said that their wishes are granted. Non-worshipers are forbidden access into the temple. Dedicating a daughter to Yellamma brings blessings to the family. The Devadasi will incarnate into a higher caste—most Devadasi are from low-caste. The higher caste society is known to buy low-caste children to dedicate to the goddess; it is auspicious, often done to undo sickness or other misfortune. An experienced Devadasi could connect to the divine simply by trance-dance or artistry. Some say they were never prostitutes but "ritual specialists". They held the highest authority of feminine divinity.

It took the power of the goddess to change the sex of a person. The wrath of the goddess comes when neglected or polluted. People with a "hot" constitution should be aware that *hunnu* (skin disease) may affect them more than others. Ayurveda, and perhaps Chinese medicine, advise these hotties to avoid things that will create more heat in the body, such as spicy food and promiscuousness.

Devadasi are considered ascetics in old age, but these women do not receive the respect once given. They are the downtrodden of Indian society. The higher castes have exploited them, in recent times, by taking advantage of these sex and agricultural workers. Once rewarded with land, that advantage slowly slipped away before the Dravidians passed the Devadasi Abolition Act in 1947 and again in 2005.

Devadasi downgraded with invaders of patriarchal religions. Patriarchal beliefs of "sex is sin" destroyed the concept of sexual equality. The culture decreed that women are householders and not likely to earn an income. The service industries have become polluted with this idea of unworthiness; the knowledge that service is sacred has gotten lost. Women in parts of Asia are considered a burden to their families. Parents of girl children, traditionally, must have a dowry to present to her suitor for marriage. In the poorest of communities, girl children may be killed at birth, sold, or given to God/Goddess.

Part 2
In the Stars

Vesta in Astrology

"Is awareness of oneself and sexuality born of shame or discretion? Without encounters with others, you cannot find yourself." - Laura Tuan.

Astrology could be transcribed as a link beween astronomy and horology—the study of space and time. An astrology chart is a stopped-clock snapshot of the cosmos.

The old symbol/glyph of Vesta is an arrow pointing down into a crevice, a lingam and yoni, an oil drill entering fractured Earth, a tree planted into Gaia, or the sacred flame radiating upward. Vesta is the ultimate self-contained devotion goddess. Initiates of Vesta are devoted to what they love and they do not give up easily. Goddess energy is the life force that all living things possess. Vesta represents strength and resolve; she changes and yet stays the same.

Vesta knows that she has a purpose, and it is not usually a romantic relationship. Relationships can cause undue stress on life when individuality has not yet developed—and when it does come to a romantic partnership, she would sooner retreat to her sacred flame than deal with an unsuitable partner who will only snuff her flame or steal her energy.

On the other hand, Vesta can become very focused on keeping a relationship alive! It is never easy for her to leave something that had so much meaning to her. Even though she knows she must move on to grow, letting a flame burn out feels like death to her. The healthiest option is to extinguish it ritually. Withdrawal is required! Her alone time is needed to cope with any unbalanced psychological process of relating. Relationships can bog her down. She must use this time to readjust her behavior or alter the relationship dynamics. Her involvement in attachment can bury her *Self* alive. She may find that she needs relationship(s) by knowing or understanding herself deeply—celibacy or unattachment is not for everyone—but she must not attach herself to someone who gets between her and her work.

Vesta contains herself well, but when she is devoted to something or someone, she is wholly (holy) faithful to them. The location of Vesta in the birth chart shows where her devotion lies. It is difficult for her to break away even when she knows she must, but her concentration is divine and she can accomplish what she needs to do.

Vesta connects us to biology, ecology, and psychology. Every one of her traits has a negative and positive side. Taken to an extreme, Vesta can have tunnel vision. Not seeing the forest through the trees, and behaving like a prude are just some of her negative traits. Giving up her position for another seems a great sacrifice, but she often does this. She can become so focused on one thing that she ignores other matters. Vesta can be selfishly self-righteous. Her focus can become her divinity without taking others into consideration. Sometimes she needs to stop and look at her surroundings to make sure nothing is catching fire. Vesta can burn herself and others without thinking twice about it. She needs to be aware of the possibility of burnout and getting burned.

Vesta, at her most positive, shows us where our purpose or divine focus is. When negative, we tend to ignore these promptings of the goddess and not be true to ourselves. Often we need to retreat when our concentration is severed, and then we can refocus ourselves on what matters most. Like the hearth, it is time to focus on the center where our flame burns. Meditation is helpful to return to our center. Art, dancing, or a stay in nature may also do the trick. Pottery making (throwing on a potter's wheel) is my go-to for fast centering.

Vesta relates to Saturn; both are responsible hard workers linked to time. Saturn re-enters a sign about every 30 years, and a Vestal's time of service was 30 years. Saturn is stern and structured, and a Vestal is learning sternness and structure.

Another similarity is that Vesta is a workaholic. Often she finds herself falling into familiar patterns of work instead of focusing on her spiritual life ... but work can be spiritual, and she can and does incorporate the two. Unfortunately, she also has too many demands on her to-do list to pay attention to them all. With devotion comes limits. Purity of intent in her actions is a key to her success.

Astrologer Demetra George popularized the concept that Vesta is the asteroid of one's Sacred Work. By "sacred work", we don't necessarily mean work that is specifically religious, just that it is the work that most feeds one's soul. When astrological clients ask what they are supposed to do with their life, some astrologers advise looking at three points: the Midheaven for practical worldly goals, the North node for long-term karmic understanding for this lifetime, and Vesta for the sacred work which will feed the soul in the meantime. If Vesta is squared or opposing one or the other two, a careful balance will have to be created. Vesta will not suffer being ignored.

Vesta knows that her desires and her growth are alone her responsibility and duty. In her community (people and politics), Vesta focuses her power on constructive social changes and transformation. She performs services to humanity and the community. She is the purifying agent and constructive force.

Vesta wants others and herself to feel safe. Threats to her life if she gives in to her sexuality do not feel safe. She understands how horrible this feeling is. As an example of Vesta's compassion, soldiers and sailors would visit the Vestals upon returning home from battle or sea. Riddled with the frightful aspects of war, Vesta offered them a safe place and a ritual of re-entrance into the civilian world.

Enough is never enough. There is always more work to be done, a constant pressure to learn, focus, and succeed. By releasing unnecessary blocks, one becomes free to experience and express their emotions. With Saturn, she is disciplined, hard-working, and may fear sex. With Venus, she may work in the sex industry and express devotion to sensual pleasures. Vesta with Mars is an extremely potent high energy that needs directing. With the Moon, it's all about emotional work, or defeating emotional inhibitions. With Vesta in Libra or the 7th temple, she is committed to her partnerships. Vesta in Taurus or the 2nd temple commits to her possessions or values. Vesta in Aquarius or the 11th temple, devoted to her humanity or her group(s). Vesta with the Sun gives monastic urges and the desire to be "spiritually special".

Vesta in the birth chart may be a place where sexual wounding has occurred. A Vesta/Chiron aspect is a good indication.

The Vesta person tends to keep to themselves. Although they often are surrounded by women or girls, they are happy keeping to themselves and do not require much unless influenced by Venus or Mars. They love life and have many, often solitary, hobbies. I would think it difficult for a Vesta person to be around people who cannot get along. They would crave their solitude! That is how they keep the fire burning: focused intent, not distracted by the everyday hustle and bustle, although they move in and out of being a part of that.

A Vestal is self-contained, but she is also capable of giving herself away too much. When she does, it is as if she is giving up her solidarity. Then it is difficult for her to focus and can cause stress or anxiety. She needs to leave her feelings outside the door of the temple, enter, and become centered.

It is one belief that Vestal Virgins were supposed to remain untouched by men. Maybe true, but modern Vestals are not without sex. If you look at the charts of those with prominent Vesta, they tend to be highly sexual. Not necessarily whores or prostitutes, but connected to their creative, sexual energy. However, it is typical for someone with a prominent Vesta to go long periods without a partner. Also, someone with a prominent Vesta can be in a relationship with someone for a long time, but may go through periods of separation or feeling unpartnered. Modern Vestals need to find ways to keep their sexual urges fed while still having their own separate lives. Vesta, in her domestic state, is the goddess who keeps the flame alive. To feed the household and keep those warm was also true of the Vestal.

Transiting Vesta changes her focus as she changes signs and houses. She entered Cancer, and the focus shifted to home, family, roots, ancestry and the karma of our ancestors, and the Moon. When she left Gemini and my 7th house/temple of partnerships, I was focusing on forming partnerships that are developing now into occult relationships (8th temple Cancer).

Someone with a prominent Vesta may experience a Vesta transit as a partnership coming to an end; then the ex-partner goes on to start a family or a lasting love relationship with another. Sometimes a Vesta-prominent person may experience her partner or partners are in love with their idealized projections of her—that is, they are not in love with her, but in who they want her to be, especially if Neptune is involved in the transit. Vesta, holding space, often allows them to do this. She can leave lovers with broken hearts when she decides to be on her own. Of course, these scenarios are interchangeable between the sexes. Whether or not the Vesta person is male or female is of little consequence.

Vesta in the Signs

Aries

Vesta in Aries is the spiritual warrior, and spiritual warriorship requires active discipline. Yoga, martial arts, or mediations in motion benefit this placement. Yoga is useful, as it requires the relaxation that this sign often takes for granted. Martial arts are great because they require the discipline that every Vesta needs. You have the creative freedom to do what you choose. Intense focus is existential for creation. When emotionally involved, an immaculate artist. You know what inspires you. Make time to sleep. Vesta requires her retreats.

The hardest part of the Aries Vesta's sacred work will be developing courage to do the right thing, and judgment to figure out what that is. It will also be finding the code of honor that is right for this work, and sticking by it.

Taurus

Vesta in Taurus has yummy physical desires. They often work with their hands creating objects from earthy materials. This is traditionally a good placement for sculptors and other three-dimensional arts, as the Taurus Vesta is ruled by Venus and Taurus is very tactile and physical. They may be controlling. Work is and should be, done the same way, every time. Conservative in the environment--natural or political--sexuality is intentionally expressed. This expression is essential for creative focus. Physical meditation includes using the body and the whole, self-awareness of your temple to sustain.

Your sacred work is something practical and body-centered, and possibly artistic; another possibility is anything to do with the Earth, ecology, and gardening. You tend to prefer working on it in a rut, in the same way every time. The more your physical needs are met, the more energy they have for their sacred work.

Gemini

Vesta in Gemini is work done over a lifetime. The lesson is to express creative ideas through intellectual art and be tested on it. It serves you not to be heartbroken if your intercommunications are not well taken or understood. Other people's conceptions are just as important and our own, and challenge your ideas to help you grow. Sometimes the only prompting needed is to clarify the thing you are trying to convey.

Focusing on a point, flame, or mandala is how you meditate. Although intellectual conversation is imperative in sexual fulfillment, too much rationalization of the emotions can lead to separation. The heart connects to the mind. Balance what you think and what you feel. Your Will is to express both your ideas and beliefs clearly. Great thoughts balance between the mind and the heart. Consider both sides as equal.

In intellectual Gemini, your sacred work is meant to be some form of communications—writing, filmmaking, speaking, teaching, some way of getting information across to the world. Vesta in Gemini feels that Information Is Sacred, because it helps us to make better choices, and free access to information is part of humanity's birthright, since discoveries do us no good if no one can find out about them. One of Gemini's challenges is healing the connection between mind and heart, and this healing may also be part of your sacred work.

Cancer

Vesta in Cancer focuses on the home and her roots. Her maternal instinct is unconditional. Sometimes her nurturing can lead to ruling over others. (I am reminded of the song Hold On Loosely by 38 Special.) Emotional attachment or nostalgia can loosen focus. Here we move into Cancer's rulership of heritage and ancestry – your sacred work has something to do with this, perhaps upholding the religion and culture of your birth, or rediscovering some older heritage and bringing it to light. The work is in the home or rediscovering your roots, family religion, or traditional heritage, but it needs to come into the present, not stay stuck in the past. You feel at home where you are needed, loved, or cherished. The sacredness of family takes presence above working for money. Smothering nurturing or feeling unloved, abandoned, or distrustful can weaken the sacred flame. Recharge with music or water.

Leo

Vesta in Leo is devoted to the service of the heart. Not always wanting to be the leader, they must hold all the pieces, parts, peoples, or tribe together. Vesta in Leo can also indicate the sacredness of leadership, taking authority in a clean and self-confident way. The trouble is the false sense of pride or ego that can develop when all eyes are on you. You must do your work not for appearances, but the sake of the whole.

Vesta in Leo is very fiery and a powerful ally to have in politics or any situation. They radiate love and have the courage of the lion. Regal in devotion, they enjoy their desires. In their cause or performance, they fight to win. Loss of focus occurs when one is only trying to impress. In Fire signs, with the bright ability to breathe life and burn the vividest, burnout often occurs. Hide away and be a child again (have some fun) and refuel your creative energy when overworked. Leo is the sign of self-expression, which indicates that this is your sacred work. You might consider writing or performing something about your own journey through life, laying it out so that others who might come through the same issues can have a place to turn.

Virgo

Vesta in Virgo is the essence of Vesta herself—the Virgin goddess in control of herself and her destiny. Vesta is at home in Virgo; it's the home sign of this reclusive, monastic asteroid that also indicates how you like to withdraw from the world. This service-oriented hermit often sacrifices herself for others and may do so happily or critically. She enjoys her work and can alienate others because of her drive to produce the very best. Her work often suppresses her spirituality. Sex, to this Vesta, is a service or a duty. Virgo is barren, but that does not mean she is not capable of fruition. She has already planned or planted her seed. Vesta is the harvester. She gathers the seeds for others to grow or eat. She knows the Earth, and she knows her body.

With Vesta in Virgo, your sacred work is in service to others, probably through doing the boring and detail-oriented tasks that they have trouble with, but which are always easier to do for others than for yourself. Vesta in Virgo may also mean that you'll be using this lifetime to sort through your feelings about your body and your health, and clean out attitudes and patterns that are bad for you. Part of your sacred work may be cleansing your flesh in this way, and making your body into a temple in a realistic way.

Libra

Vesta in Libra signifies someone more focused on others than they are themselves. Each partnership is a gift from God/Goddess. Trouble in relationships when the native focuses only on pleasing the other. They often sacrifice for the partner or relationships. With an exchange, a balance of give-and-take is necessary.

Vesta in Libra puts the sacred work in either the work of justice or the work of beauty and harmony—the path of the white knight or the path of the artist. Equality, law, and justice are often the focus. Venus' influence brings tremendous artistic and creative abilities—art in the home, perhaps interior design. Their art, sex, or what they create, their sacred fire, is tied to their spiritual work. Although they often desire to work in/with groups, their clinginess and constant need for approval and competition may annoy or drive others away. She needs to learn to sit with herself. At her best, she brings peace and serenity to her sacred space and friendships. Sexuality becomes contained when one searches for higher truth. Her energy is then refined and genuinely expressed. When used for higher aspirations, beauty and love radiate.

If partnerships may be a source of unhappiness, this Vesta will learn to love their work. The Libra Vesta may finds themselves surrounded by lawbreakers in order to learn forgiveness. On the other hand, Vesta in the sign of partnership indicates that your sacred work is best done in conjunction with someone else, perhaps as part of a small team or two or three. Comparing yourself to other people is the downfall of this sign, as it riles up a competitive streak and drags down the cooperation needed to do this work.

Scorpio

Vesta in Scorpio is sexy! She must express herself sexually. Exploring sexuality allows for growth. Sex is sacred, and it does you well to treat it as such. Trust is a must to enter your sacred space; sexual intensity requires an open and honest relationship. Your focus is disturbed when you feel guilt, shame, or sin for your experiences. Repression of self leads to regression of self—everything has an underlying meaning. The Scorpio Vesta may be very judgmental. Scorpio has the most intense emotions of all the signs, and Vesta here also suggests that your sacred work may be centered around understanding and mastering your negative emotions. With Vesta in Scorpio, the Will is so strong that one can overcome the negative feelings or emotions through her sacred fire. Burn them off and rise again. Abstinence or reclusion are ways to cleanse and recharge your energy.

Sagittarius

Your focus, and your sacred work, is on finding the Truth. That's a tricky thing, capital-T truth, because most of the people who've gone looking for it have either found what they thought was Truth, and ended up in back alleyways of intolerance and dogmatism ... or they've found that the only Truth is that there are many different truths. You may learn that truth is subjective; to each their own. Loss of focus happens when one becomes dogmatic or takes their views to be the only one true religion. But it is the cause, purpose, or beliefs/ideas that motivate your creative energies. Seeking and experiencing extravagant adventures (physical or nonphysical) gets your juices flowing. Your practical approach will move the world. Mahatma Gandhi had Vesta in

Sagittarius; he was married but celibate for many years, and encouraged others to be so as well. Celibacy is not uncommon for this sign as they use their sacred fire for achieving their desire. Truth and the temple of Vesta resides inside.

Capricorn

Vesta in Capricorn has the Will to succeed. Involvement in business and politics (personal or worldly) is likely. Although loyal to tradition and the status quo, they are often in positions of authority. Capricorn is the sign of ambition and discipline, and this placement suggests that you are supposed to learn to discipline yourself by any means necessary, and then use that discipline to help others – perhaps teaching them about how to do it, perhaps using it to get things done in the world. Your sacred work may take you into a position of authority, and you may have to learn about how to do that with integrity and honor. However, since Vesta also rules our need for solitude, you may need to take periodic breaks from being in charge in order to refresh your perspective. Once disciplined, you can move up the ladder by teaching others what you have learned. When safe and secure in honest commitment, your fire burns brightest.

Aquarius

Vesta in Aquarius brings in the new. Sometimes this placement represents the underdog to lift others. Danger may occur if the focus becomes overly thrown into the future; reckless behavior should be thwarted. Any rebellion, to work in your favor, requires proper planning. Take time to enjoy the present moment; Uranus and Saturn are both present in this placement. This Vesta is inventive and freedom-loving and political and business-oriented. Aquarius is ruled by nonconforming Uranus, so your sacred work will be found in introducing new and unusual things to people. It could also be working with humanitarian organizations or goals. Vesta in Aquarius goes back and forth between wanting lots of solitude, and wanting lots of people to be around. It may be difficult for you to gauge what level of social stimulation you need, before you burn out.

This is the sister that starts reforms and changes minds. Quick meditations throughout the day, tapping the thymus, for example, bring one into the present moment, are recommended to avoid burnout. Studying astrology transits is also helpful to recognize your patterns. For example: Emphasis in your 12th house/temple by transits may be a time better spent alone or only with a select individual. Owning a vivacious nature lets all enter your sacred space—with boundaries, of course!

Pisces

Your sacred work is developing compassion for others; sometimes it can be about sacrificing oneself in order to take care of someone who is ill, or working in confined institutions with the patients or prisoners. Whatever the work turns out to be, it is part of the difficult path of learning compassion for other beings. Because Pisces is such a subjective sign, this path needs to be blindly experienced as it comes rather than being actively pursued. If you wait, it will come to you; your job is to welcome it when it comes and be open to making the sacrifice that will teach you so much. Your focus is going with the flow. Poetic and inconsistent, the way you control the sacrosanct is by taking it as it comes and knowing intuitively when it is appropriate to act. Focus can be difficult for this placement. Dreams can be a source of inspiration, meditation, and healing. In politics, you play the martyr to gain influence. Spirituality may come from the Tantric tradition. Your healing touch is available to those that seek it. Celibacy may come at times to those inclined in the spiritual practice—Vesta in Pisces has a monastic feeling to its energy—or possibly using sex to heal others.

Vesta in the Houses/Temples

1st Temple

Vesta, positioned in the first house/temple, has the Will to create through self, catalyzing, sustaining, or destroying. Devote your sacred energy to your highest, Will, and you will fulfill your Vesta role. However, devotion to the self can make you radically closed off to developing long-term relationships with others. Your self-knowledge and independence attract others. It feels secure in the self-contained space that you provide, but it also makes it impossible to get closer to you. The discipline comes in sacrificing relationships by focusing on ideas, dreams, and aspirations. Achieving them is your goal and you will not settle for less. The danger is when you do not live up to your high expectations of yourself. Rome did not finish in a day. Take a rest and try again when you have restored your creative energies.

Vesta is in the 1st to test the ego. Vesta's Will is personal self-discovery. Sacrifice and healing come in relating. Vesta in the 1st house/temple has no problem burning off relations. Your sacred space is your personal space which typically gets shared with no one. Your purity radiates so well that others feel it would be violating to touch you. Since the first house is also linked to identity, and Vesta is purity, you are very critical of yourself and how you come across. You hold yourself to a high standard of presentation and can feel insecure when you don't live up to it. Your appearance is your devotion, and you set examples for how other Vestals should appear. Self-development is your sacred work.

In synastry: Your Vesta in someone else's 1st house/temple implies expressed devotion and shared interest. It may feel like something is lacking, but figuring that out may be beneficial to growth. Purity is part of the equation, and you can inspire them to purify their appearance or their ideas around how they should present themselves.

2nd Temple

Vesta is a resource, and Vesta values purity. The Will requires the best of the best; the second house/temple sets restrictions and tests the Vestal. They may even deny the things they value. Having their own source of income is extremely important for this placement. They may devote themselves to stockpiling resources, preserving the created. Healing comes when resources and energy exchange is engaged. Often our best works come straight out of our creative fire and from the goddess herself. What is that worth? Value the sacred.

Thrifty to a fault, Vesta in the 2nd temple knows the importance of conserving resources. How one uses resources is invaluable, and Vesta will test on that. Sometimes all one needs to do is change their perspective. Vesta here talks about values, and it's your sacred job to find worthy ones. What would you sell, and for how much, and what parts of you cannot be bought? These are questions you will need to work out for yourself, and doing so is very important to your life. You may need to work on cleansing your attitudes toward money and possessions, and may even need to have periods where you give everything away or live on very little, in order to remind yourself what is most important in life. Money is energy, and commerce is just as vital as other energy. How much does one put into work, and how much comes out? Restriction may occur in growth and fruitfulness as lessons on learning how to manifest the Will or focus.

In synastry: If your Vesta is in another's 2nd temple, you will share your resources when resources are low. You may deny yourself material pleasures or give too much of them away. You open your sacred space to those in need of the protection of the hearth and home.

3rd Temple

Vesta located in the 3rd house/temple periodically pulls away from their relationships to go within. They often live with "brothers or sisters" or dedicate themselves to institutions which develop one's mind. Sexual relationships will be heavily intellectually scrutinized, and perhaps "mined" for stories, as this Vesta is a storyteller.

Your sacred work is done with words. The inspiring intellect, the teacher, scholar, or scribe in the community; she uses her words to convey information. Your work is to project what is dear to your soul through public speaking or professional writing. Journaling is a psychological tool and becomes a representation of the times, recording history in the making. Youngsters with this placement should be encouraged to take up creative writing. Community is sacred to you.

In synastry: If your Vesta is in another's 3rd temple, you will help them to bring clarity to their words. You may worry that their friends or family will not accept you. You may provide them with friendship or an intellectual aid through personal training, school, or career.

4th Temple

Vesta in the 4th house/temple transcends beliefs set or patterned through the parents or home life. They maintain, create, or liberate ancestral heritage, right or wrong. Vesta in the home sets fire to purify beliefs on ethics.

Vesta in the 4th temple focuses on the home and family; it is their duty and sacred work. Housecleaning is a meaningful meditation, including removing outdated or toxic material from time and traditions past. The most important part of the sacred work is to learn how to have a good attitude about taking care of family, and never let resentment get the better of you. This temple is the root, and Vesta is known to change families. She is a nymph by day and a tree by night; she may wander around in the Sun and returns to the Earth by the moonlight. She may realize that a tree needs its roots grounded in the Earth to thrive. Her familiar environment is sacred.

In synastry: Your Vesta in another's 4th temple represents empathy. You provide the space needed for higher purposes or sacrifices. Practicing non-attachment or other occult matters includes the changing or isolation from family.

5th Temple

Love of Life! Sex and the creative inspiration that comes from it is their focus. They lose themselves in the creative impulses which are their sacred work. Doubt has disappeared, and Vesta can act free through and within herself. She may have trouble with romantic boundaries and find no difference between herself and the other she wants to merge with. The key is learning to open the heart in a transpersonal way even when there is pain on a personal level, while holding clear boundaries.

This Vesta is often childless, or is separated from their children by circumstances in their early years, and may only have children late in life if at all. Vesta in the 5th temple is a risk-taker. Their focus is on their creativity, but the mind and heart must strive to remain positive. Too much focus on the negative kills the consecrated energy. Take time to play by yourself. This Vesta's sacred service belongs to the "children" made by their creative power and given to the world.

In synastry: Your Vesta in their 5th temple may restrict their creative expression if they take life too seriously or experience jealousy. Children or creative projects may be stalled or even denied. Priorities, including children or past relationships, may cause separation. Awareness of both your childlike natures allows some understanding.

6th Temple

Vesta in the 6th house/temple heals through her acts of service, and service is her sacred work. She is open to anyone who seeks healing. If free to live how she chooses, she serves all without discrimination. She is fully present in her experiences with her craft.

Sacred service initiates, they may work in the service industry, health care and medicine, hospitality industry, or in an institutional setting. Vesta in the 6th temple will work creatively, endlessly, or without reward or recognition; they are dedicated to the service and not the accolades. It's important to acquire the proper nutrients to turn into energy. Mentoring others may also be important on your quest. If you start rendering service with a bad attitude, however, take a break from it until you are ready to do it with a whole heart again. This Vesta's health and wellness, work, or time, is her sacred service.

In synastry: With your Vesta in their 6th temple, you may deny yourself in this relationship. You may feel you need to provide a service for them or heal them in some way. You may give them the space needed to understand their Vestal work.

7th Temple

This Vesta's focus is on resolving conflict. However, their aspirations may be lost as knowledge emerges through human contact and understanding. They work best with a partner, friend, or adversary.

Vesta placed in the seventh temple has difficulty in their sacred work since it involves another. They must learn that their spiritual work is theirs and theirs alone, but at the same time a suitable partnership may be essential for their divine pursuit. Their focus is the relationship between self and the other; the most spiritual work they will do is the effort to achieve a deep and spiritually committed relationship. The lesson is learning to work together to achieve the compassion and empathy of relating, and the deep sea of wealth and happiness that a committed partnership can create. Be aware of an inappropriate partner pulling you away from that sacred work. If weak, this Vesta may try to put her work onto the partner; she must put in the effort herself. The adversary may appear in partnerships as a challenge. This Vesta's spiritual service is relating and diplomacy.

In synastry: With your Vesta in their 7th temple, you enhance their public reputation. In marriage, you have a tendency to deny or get rejected from complete fulfillment as you are also adversaries, but you have the potential to teach them about spiritual relationship when you have learned that lesson yourself. Your emphasis on their responsibilities adds to their workload.

8th Temple

This Vesta may lose themselves in the occult by gaining supreme knowledge through universal consciousness. They are rarely satiated or satisfied with the exchange of others. Devotion lies in the unattainable and indefinable. This Vesta's acquiring of knowledge and experience is her sacred Will.

Vesta in the 8th temple is about profound transformation, especially around the areas of sexuality, the attitude towards death, and sharing finances. Your sacred work is to transform these areas within yourself until there are no impure motivations, and you can be clean about them all. Until then, you may go through crises and power struggles in these areas, which is the Universe's way of drawing attention to them. Relationships can be soul-deep, and she may find that not many share in her intensity surrounding taboo subjects. The lesson is to let go of impurities. She may feel that the partner does not meet all her needs, and that is all right—share with them anyway, and be pure enough for all who share her sacred space. If there are problems, take time to hide away, keep your finances separate, or be celibate for a time. Clear the sacred space and be one—whole in yourself—until you feel clean again.

In synastry: With your Vesta in their 8th temple, your ideals are often unfulfilled. You do not like your partner spending shared money, or you do not like how they spend it; both of you need to work on purifying your attitudes towards resources and their use. You may spark an interest in taboo sex, death, or the occult in them.

9th Temple

Vesta in the 9th house/temple finds the spirit in the here and now. They may have a devotion to higher education, foreign lands, or philosophy. Pilgrimage may be their main religious devotion. Vesta in the 9th temple may limit growth if one becomes stuck in her beliefs to the point of bias or extremism. They may be convinced they have the true and only way, and then they fall into trouble. At their best, they bring together people of different cultures and beliefs, and share truth and wisdom. Every time they find themselves denying the beliefs of others, they should study them and find a middle ground. Knowledge is their sacred space.

In synastry: With your Vesta in their 9th temple, you may help to unravel their world view or way of thinking. Trips may be delayed or canceled. Questioning beliefs can strengthen or tear them down, but it's good if you share the same philosophies or faiths.

10th Temple

A spiritual devotion through vocation turns knowledge into wisdom. She is time, and she transcends time; the reflection of all who are entranced by her independence. Duality to the ignorant, one within herself to the wise. The mother and the father. This Vesta's career, ambition, or life path is her spiritual Will.

Vesta in the 10th temple makes her sacred work into a worldly career, sometimes to the point that it becomes more of a sacrifice than a billion-dollar scheme, but she has the discipline required to see it through. Career success may not manifest until she reaches a certain point of personal maturity and growth, emotionally and spiritually; in the meantime, the trap is grasping at the wrong career and getting trapped. Vesta conjunct the MC means sacred work is her destiny. They may give more than they receive and are prone to workaholism. It is wise to schedule regular breaks.

In synastry: With your Vesta in their 10th temple, you may follow them down a rabbit hole or perhaps enjoy the journey they take you on. You may delay their success or make them rethink their career choices. Sharing your sacred place is not something you do swiftly with them, but you let them know they are needed.

11th Temple

Through friendships, she finds herself. This Vesta understands universal consciousness and the brotherhood/sisterhood of all. She connects with all others through the mind and change happens on a social level. Group gatherings and humanitarian projects call to her, and are her sacred work, as is purifying her attitudes about friendship, being part of a group, and social approval.

Vesta in the 11th temple sacrifices herself for humanity. When the tribe becomes too much, she retreats to sanctuary. Learning how to work in groups is a life lesson, often sacrificing oneself for friends or worthy causes. When focused, she works for the highest goal. She may rely on a strong code of ethics so as not to be taken for a ride.

In synastry: When your Vesta is in their 11th temple, you may bring out their humanitarian side. This is a good interaspect for deep friendship and you will stick by them no matter what. You may be too trusting with them, however. This Vesta temple protects the sacred spaces of the Earth.

12th Temple

Vesta in the 12th temple prefers isolation. This is someone with the soul of a nun or internal virgin, although they may sometimes merge with the outer world to bring it within for total realization. This Vesta's sovereignty or isolation is her Will.

The 12th temple is often the place of dreams and sometimes secrets you do not want to tell, even yourself. Vesta in the 12th represents occult affairs, confinement, isolation; healing occurs when taboos around these areas are accepted. Her sacred work may be wound up in places of confinement—hospitals, prisons, working with shut-ins, etc. The 12th is also the house of psychology and the unconscious, so the sacred work may involve using faith to help overcome fear. Removing distractions and making a space of clean simplicity helps. Awareness of your physical disabilities is a must when working with Vesta in the 12th temple. Understand why this limitation is there, and grow higher in spirituality.

In synastry: With your Vesta in their 12th temple, you may enjoy hiding out together, or you may separate in some way (a long-distance relationship or astral plane connection). There is a psychic or otherworldly connection, and you help them to purify their unconscious. This placement encourages spiritual highs and the energy for psychological growth.

The Vesta Forum: Aspects

Vesta/Sun

Sacred work is self-actualization or the finding of oneself; whatever is chosen as this work, it becomes the very identity by which you define yourself. The conjunction is the placement of devoting yourself entirely to Spirit, and is also a mark of the discipline's path. Challenging aspects may find you fighting against the sacred work in order to keep your identity, but eventually you must become who you need to be in order to merge with it. The focus of Vesta concentrates on what one is in a physical, spiritual essence. This is the Keeper of the Eternal Flame.

Your father may have been a workaholic and modeled self-discipline for you, or been enough of a problem that you had to learn self-discipline to manage. You may feel more welcome at work than at home, and may feel most secure there.

Those with Vesta in the Sun's forum may appear selfish in ways that alienate others. This forum may keep her fire so hot that it burns when one comes too close. Taming the fire is necessary, but it will always be ablaze. Relationships may feel too restricting for this independent virgin, but a lesson to learn is that others often help us to understand and grow our selves.

Recognize the spiritual work as *the* work. It may not always look the way you want to see it, but you can change that. Tune and control the fire to the heart of hearts. The power is within you.

Vesta/Moon

Mothering, caretaking, divination, or spiritual nourishment is the sacred work. Focused discipline on internal emotions helps one feel secure in their vessel. Cooking and preparing food is a source of nourishment and natural healing. A conjunction to the Moon is a high placement for Vesta, typical of Vestals or nuns and monks. Continually purifying an internal devotion will be your personal discipline.

Detachment from emotional relationships or physical or spiritual nourishment in stressful forums indicates a possible denial of mother issues. Your mother may have worked or tended to be high-strung, negligent, or passive, and did not give you a good role model for expressing healthy emotions; part of the sacred work may be learning to do that. These aspects can indicate infertility or work that tears them away from family or emotional connections.

The Vesta/Moon forum emotes their spiritual, sexual, or political beliefs socially, and do best when relying on intuition rather than intellect. Working spiritually with good mother figures or being taught spirituality by mothers is a natural thing. The ability to focus on a single thought is excellent, but may alienate you from the rest of the world. With a harmonious forum, they can see past emotions and love all types of people no matter their own emotional state, or that of the people in front of them. The calming waters of the moon draw many to bath in the depth and beauty of this Vesta.

Vesta/Mercury

Vesta in the forum of Mercury sanctifies communication. When young, they may doubt their speaking or writing skills, but the lesson is to take time to clarify. Mercury prefers to be swift, but takes time to learn a language or how to organize and cleanse the thoughts. The Vesta/Mercury forum must take time to learn, including learning to cleanse the thought processes of constant negativity. They experience life from a detached viewpoint. This Vesta may possess the ability to speak directly to Deity, as Mercury is the messenger between the Earth and god/goddess. This forum may also occur as ease of communication with the higher self. The more one expresses the sacred work through words, the more one purifies the spiritual fire and focuses on the path.

The unhealthy manifestation may find communication difficult or may lead to troublesome arguments or mental unreliability. Too much or too little introspection fogs the creation. Meditation in motion focuses the mind and the body. Doubt is the worst enemy. Worry is useless energy unless one can do something about it. For clarity, let go of the stress by focusing on the present moment. Clarity brings balance to the point where even the mundane becomes spiritualized. Lighten up and study or share in spiritual experiences.

The harmonious forum of Vesta/Mercury is a mind attuned and directed to ideas or ideals. Part of the sacred work to others belongs in the area of teaching. Teaching, writing, speaking from research, divine encounters, or other media, is her path. When guiding others through instruction, she is the lighthouse; the fountain of wisdom flows through the temple.

Vesta/Venus

This forum represents the virgin lover, sexuality, and purity in dispute. They may struggle with dissonance in beliefs—what they have learned about sex and what they want to explore may be on separate ends of the spectrum, and frigidity in intimacy may result. The key is learning that sacredness in sexuality is about seeing the other person as a sacred being, not what acts are done together. Creative projects tend to be worked alone, unless other factors in the chart suggest group work. The sacred space is wrapped up in the pleasures of the physical world or earning money and recognition. As we grow wiser, we understand that even the physical world is sacred and spiritual. Let curiosity lead. Masturbation may come to be used as a source of inspiration.

Vesta/Venus in an unhealthy manifestation may have to choose between love and her sacred work, which is usually a Venusian art she focuses on. Either path is difficult, but there is a choice. The artist may often need to work alone, so setting boundaries allows relationships and personal work to balance the need for independence and passionate relationships. When manifesting harmoniously, this Vesta understands the psychology of relationships and the importance of having a clean slate for working. Part of this sacred work is the art of relating; sex transmutes into artistic creations. Love is the expression of an artist! The lesson may come in developing sexual preferences and limitations.

Vesta/Mars

The Vesta/Mars forum packs a powerful punch! This is the mark of the sacred warrior, and the energy may best move through martial arts, activism, and defending the sacred. This Vesta has the power of assertion and Will, and possesses the masculine energy to direct her focus where she sees the need. She dares to stand in battle and by duty defend her sanctuary.

Challenging aspects can manifest as someone who rejects the spiritual warrior role because they are busy defending the innocents. They are not warlike, but may offer an out to those caught up in war (physical or psychological). Overaggressive sexuality can cause problems in intimate relationships. Often seen as an object of desire, this forum is easily frustrated, and the lesson is gaining control of personal power. Reacting with anger is disempowering. Standing up for others is as crucial as the power to protect the sacred self. An unhealthy manifestation can also appear as the need for independence rebelling against the duty to the sacred work. Once they have integrated and clearly understands their path, they have the potential to align their focus and drive their will to their purpose and duty.

The harmonious forum is a true warrior—not necessarily military, but a fighter for what is sacred, with strong activist or political motivations. Alignment with oneness drives the spiritual goals and aspirations. Sexual energy may concentrate into an expression of a cause.

Vesta/Ceres

The spiritual work is in nature and nurture. They may have learned through a death-like experience how to nurture other natural beings. This forum radiates mother-goddess energy. The sacred work is in the garden, the kitchen, and nurturing Earth where and when needed. It may also be in cleansing the heart of old wounds around inadequate nurturing through spiritual connection.

In times of stress, they may take on too much work in caring for others, so boundaries need to be set on sacred time and resources.

Drama and family demands may pull her away from her highest work that needs time to accomplish. This forum can sometimes indicate infertility, or the need to escape from family demands through work. Alone time is required.

In times of harmony, they are committed to the family. To Vesta, however, that is often her chosen or adopted family. Spiritual nurturing and service to her adopted family connect her to her work. The lesson is accepting the past and creating a better future in the natural, loving world.

Vesta/ Pallas

This forum bestows focused planning and organized strategizing. Although they may be highly sexed, they need to put priorities (sacred work) ahead of relationships. Pallas and Vesta both have "daddy" issues, and the lesson is independence in creativity. In fact, the most common manifestation of this forum is that the sacred work is the creative work, and dedicating oneself to it heals all. The knowledge of the path begins with the joy of experiencing.

These two goddess asteroids are the most connected to both their feminine and masculine personality. Together, this suggests that another manifestation of the sacred work may be experiencing life as transgender or asexual, sometimes sexually non-penetrative. (The level of sexuality depends on the signs and aspects the planets make. Scorpio is more sexual than Aquarius, for example.) Gender expression corresponds to self-integration, and this forum may lean towards political work around gender, bringing together the two extremes.

When stressed, this forum may have trouble linking the sacral and the crown. This imbalance can create social or political issues which alienate from intimate relationships. Sometimes desire and duty square off inside the mind/body. The lesson lies in making a decision and focusing on the chosen path. Allow room for a change of mind. Seek and learn what you have to in order to bring the political and spiritual together into one goal. Take time to strengthen or clear out that belief system. Also, Vesta is the asteroid of focus and Pallas is the asteroid of recognizing patterns, and if the forum is stressed there can be neurological problems around this.

Vesta/Hygiea

The sacred work lies in the unseen health precautions. The work you do may go unnoticed but not unfelt. They may work in a sanitation position, such as cleaning and prepping before a meal or surgery. Devotion to personal hygiene is a sacred priority.

When stressed, you may be a "neat freak". Fear of sickness may lead to intimacy alienation. There is a risk of being hurt on the job, or working in unsanitary conditions. The challenge is understanding hurt or past/present/future sickness, so one may understand how to prevent these ills in themselves and others. The spiritual work lies in cleaning out our sacred space and preserving the wellbeing of self and others.

In harmony, this forum takes precautions against what ails them. A keen sense of noticing hygienic practices may keep them safe from the unclean. The sacred work involves protecting others from infections or injuries by keeping the workplace free of debris and well stocked with healing waters, potions, and herbal essences.

Vesta/Juno

This forum is a zealot in the political sense and may focus on record or contract keeping. They may save emails, text messages, and receipts. Keeping track is the sacred work and the duty. This forum is beneficial in relationships to keep things fair and equal. In synastry, this forum has the potential for an artistic or political workmate.

A stressful forum is a difficult path between sovereignty and the marriage contract. Fulfilling the sacred arrangement may be interrupted by an obligation to another. Often one surrenders to the partner to hold her position. She may love the romantic game but desires to be on her path. The lesson may be in finding a partner supportive of her individual karmic requirements, as well as purifying such relationship obstacles as jealousy, insecurity, manipulation, codependence, and poor boundaries.

When harmonious, Vesta is interested in relating to others by knowing herself. By knowing herself, she may find a suitable partnership before a contract is signed. Her internal balance draws supportive partnerships who help create the sacred work, and attracts like-minded individuals easily, forging spiritually fulfilling relationships brought together by contracts, karma, or dedication.

Vesta/Jupiter

Your very nature is to seek knowledge whenever possible, and you can see the light at the end of the tunnel when everyone else misses it. The sacred work may be in religion, philosophy, higher education, or teaching. Vesta and Jupiter work well together, as learning about others advances one's spirituality. You love exploring the way people think, behave, and believe. By allowing the views of others to come into focus, you can improve how you teach. Gardner's *Theory of Multiple Intelligences* is a recommended study.

When stressed, they may be overly involved in their work, as Jupiter is overdoing. Out of all Vesta placements, this is the one most prone to burnout. When involved in work, they may need reminding several times a day to take a break. Ask people for reminders or set alarms for breaks and meals, as trying to overdo tends to make it impossible to deliver on time. Vesta is so involved with focusing on spiritual devotion that social and sexual relationships are feared or pushed to the back burner. Take time often to look around and see how others are responding, and check in with them from time to time.

Harmonious aspects allow this Vesta to travel physically or mentally. She is the seeker of truth and spiritual intuition. Her sexual power is strong, and she is able to control a room of politicians. She deals with the world on a larger scale; the sacred path is of the advanced educator. She does her work through publishing or scribing the various views of the world.

Vesta/Saturn

The Saturn/Vesta forum is highly disciplined. Hard work and a rough life pushes them to become refined. The sacred work may involve alchemy, turning lead into diamonds. Saturn contracts and crystallizes, so purifying the self with practice and restrictions allows one to concentrate on the hard work before rest or death. This forum can indicate that they will not come fully to their sacred work until old age, or at least until the second Saturn return. It can also indicate a role of spiritual authority, and the ability to apply practical common sense and honest logic to spirituality.

The stressful forum of Vesta/Saturn causes tensions between the sacred work and the mundane. Responsibilities of the world, distractions from ambitious projects, and boredom create a wandering mind and soul. The focus returns to love. When work becomes too much, take a break to enjoy and refresh. Bringing awareness to the present moment helps one to stay centered. Balancing responsibilities with fulfillment of the sacred is the work.

When harmonious, this forum gives the ability and commitment to perform the sacred work. Purposeful and intense, Vesta/Saturn offers the realization of vision. Surrender occurs and builds confidence toward pressure. Work is life; everything is godly, even restrictions and household chores.

Vesta/Chiron

Wounds of the temple, spiritual or sexual, leads one to the sacred path of one's spiritual healing. A higher understanding of Chiron teaches that pain is part of the healing process. One would not be the same without it. Self-care becomes whole-care and eventually extends to others. Vesta is the work that the knife or sword will do; Chiron is the pounding on the anvil that got it that way.

When stressed, this forum requires separation from other(s) to find integration within the self. The sacred space is where healing work begins, but challenges may block the path. Trouble facing the wounds or scars can sabotage the work one wants to undergo and do diligently.

Face the issue head-on and get to the underlining cause of the matter. Prayer and devotion help to alleviate the pain of dealing with deep cuts or scars. Remember to be patient with yourself.

When harmonious, this forum connects the need to heal the self as part of the sacred work. You may recognize the wounds of others and be able to help them based on personal experiences. This understanding allows for more knowledge about the self and uses self-healing to teach others the sacred art.

Vesta/Uranus

The sacred work of this forum is information. Intuition leads one to find the path. Astrology, the internet, and electronics are teaching tools; intuitive and highly scientific Vesta/Uranus finds the new and deconstructs popular belief, challenging social mores and being a model of individuality. This forum advances humankind in politics, activism, and natural sciences. The point is not to deliberately shock or challenge, nor to be the spiritual thrillseeker, but to pursue the path and not be turned aside by social demands or shaming.

When chaos ensues, this forum focuses on sacred personal work and on doing whatever comes. They may have unusual sexual or relationship practices, or they may be a repressed prude. The lesson is in revolutionizing change to build up or tear down whenever necessary. The more they question what they were taught early on, the more their path will come into focus.

When love ensues, the mind is focused, and creative innovation leads the way to elevated vision. The path alone can be rebellious and throw off social norms; you may have clashes between traditional spirituality and what speaks to you personally. Keep walking the unique path even if people are gawking.

Vesta/Neptune

These are the artists and magicians, as well as the monks and nuns; their creativity pulls from the endless cosmic understanding. Closing yourself off to go within is the sacred path of this forum. It is the spiritual, internal, and eternal work. This forum is less about service and more about contemplation, at least at first. Service will come when compassion is deeply learned.

If stressed, this forum may experience confusion about sacred work. What is ethereal, and what is astral? Vesta/Neptune people may be the type to fall asleep on her watch or daydream instead of work. Sometimes it is easier to dream than look at the reality of one's world, as Neptune is the escapist, martyr, and mystic; dreamy and magical. They may punish themselves unnecessarily, or sacrifice for unworthy reasons. This sacred path links the physical plane where one takes form to the seven other planes of existence: red, orange, yellow, green, blue, indigo, and violet.

When harmonious, this is the sacred forum of pure spirituality—the white light, the contemplative monk/nun. To progress, they need commitment and discipline to an ideal or an art that arises from spiritual encounters. They long for the sacred, although the desire or longing may disrupt work or relationships. Sexual union may be part of the path, although it may not be physical. Disappointment may arise when partners turn out to be mere mortals instead of divine beings, and they may have trouble reconciling spirituality with earthy sex. It will be important for them to learn that a spiritual union can also involve bodies and hearts.

Vesta/Pluto

The Vesta/Pluto forum has a deep well of passion and drive for spiritual development. It is the sign of the indifferent yogi undisturbed by outside circumstances. They handle upheavals in a calm manner, although fear of sex or one's sexual nature is typical. This forum seeks transcendence through sex, death, and rebirth.

Part of this sacred path requires sex, so they often seek sexual fulfillment through others because of the need for transcendence. Although their real route to enlightenment is through the self. Masturbation has a way of healing sexual, emotional, psychological, pain, manipulation, or other transgressions/obsessions. Purifying the sexuality is an important part of the path, and can indicate periods of celibacy for cleansing purposes. They need to make a commitment to find out what sex looks like when it is done cleanly on all levels. They may work with Tantra, sex magic, or become the lover of a deity or spirit. Dark mysteries beckon to them, and they may be frightened of where their spiritual path leads. It is important to understand that to the pure, all things are pure.

When stressed, issues between personal power and sacred work occur. They may feel that holding on to power or giving their power away to another is blocking personal or spiritual development. Balance may be required. Setting and breaking boundaries even for oneself is possible. How much energy contributes to focused transcendence versus how much energy conserved for others? This forum can move mountains through creation or destruction, and can center around redemption for past dark deeds.

In harmony, it is all or nothing. Strong Vesta urges us to go deeper into exploration. She loves an investigation. It is in the dark that one finds the light. Curiosity of the occult leads to frightening yet powerful results; focused energy leads to high performances. This forum may use the sexual prowess of Pluto in politics for social causes. The sacred path is physical, spiritual, and perhaps social transformation. Dedication to a time of celibacy or self-love heals, renews, and rejuvenates.

Vesta/Eris

This forum raises hell to push for social and political change. Family or society, drama, or dysfunction; she is the sexy taboo that people may try to stay clear of. However, angrily turning away from others may create chaos in the work and relationship space. This Vesta makes a stand in the community; she can be the sexual temptress or the resentful hermit. Chaos does not have to result, although it usually does.

Vesta/Nodes or MC

This forum exhibits a strong emphasis on work. What is found through the divine work controls the outcome of who you know, where you go, and how you grow. When stressed, take a break and enjoy a social event. Relationships may suffer due to the time and energy one places on work, especially when Vesta is on the MC.

Vesta in the forum of the Nodes is positive when manifesting in a healthy way, because it indicates that the sacred work and the karmic path are in harmony, and perhaps one and the same. Challenging aspects can indicate a conflict between the two, and a careful balance is required. This is especially difficult when both are important spiritual goals.

Vesta/Ascendant

Your sacred work is being who you are, where everyone can see it. The focus is on the temple or home. She may not want her sacred work to be embodying the domestic goddess, but when the focus is on herself and her temple, her sacredness is enhanced. Her focus on her work may be perceived as selfishness by her family. On the other hand, the general demeanor lends itself to aiding with the sacred work, because people trust you to do what you say. Hard work and self-sacrifice allow for personal sacred space and holy matrimony to take place.

Vesta Retrograde

Vesta is retrograde about three months for each year. Retrogrades often allow us to review our work and time. Vesta retrograde is true to that. Busy with work or unmotivated. She represents the wintertime tree--roots: sinking sap deep into the taproot. The need to go inside while having to be active. Laziness and the need to meditate and center. Finding your center. A search for the light in the dark. Activism takes her focus away from her work.

Nikola Tesla: an example of Vesta in the 2nd Temple.

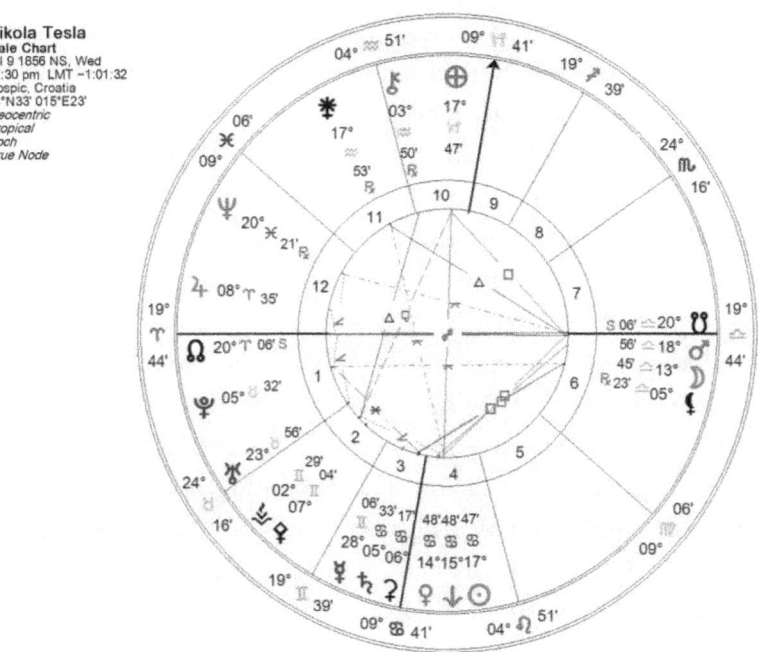

When the exact time is unknown, astrologers often use the Aries point, the Sun, North Node, or noon/midnight as the rising (ascendant). Nikola Tesla's birth chart is a good example. The theory is that Tesla was born at midnight during a lightning storm. I am using the 11:30 pm chart because of what I know of Tesla. The North Node would be appropriate in the 1st or 12th temple; however, given his aversion to relationships, the South Node would likely be in the 7th temple. Also, his Sun in the 4th temple is on the Imum Coeli (IC) or nadir in the midnight chart. Imum Coeli is Latin for "bottom of the sky". In the 11:30 pm chart, Ceres and Venus are closest to the IC., considered weak on this point. Also, the midnight chart puts Pluto on the Ascendant. Given what I know of Tesla, he is more of a visionary and a doer (North Node rising) than a sexy control freak (Pluto rising), although controlling his sexuality is a part of his nature,. He was never known to have physical relationships with women, and a rumor said he was repulsed by women who wore pearls. Pearls have a long-held symbolical link to Aphrodite, the goddess of love, and represent the bride or marriage.

To accomplish great things, he knew he had to retain his power. Spirituality nurtured him, and he enjoyed sharing spirituality and scientific knowledge with others. With Pluto in his first house, he often fell ill in his youth, but it gave him the power to transform. With Vesta in his second temple of values, he valued his alone time. Close to Pallas, he was very independent.

Nikola Tesla has Vesta trine Chiron. His most painful hurt was not fulfilling his greatest goal: to light up the Earth with a second Sun or bring free energy to all of humanity. With a semi-square to his Sun, his work was his fire. It is what fueled him.

Known as a famous scientist and "the father of the alternating current", Nikola Tesla was also an astrologer and a very spiritual man. "The first requirement is a high awareness of your mission and the work to be done ... The oak knows that it is an oak tree ...The second condition to adapt is determination. All I could, I finished it." (*Everything is Light*, the Incredible interview with Nikola Tesla.)

Electricity is a cosmic energy. The Law of Attraction, together with Coulomb's Law (repulsion), creates electricity when brought through a medium such as a light bulb or a lit oven. Like merging the things we like and dislike about ourselves into a 3rd or unified whole, this center pole holds these oppositions in harmony.

The Vesta Discovery Chart

Vesta is a minor planet located in the asteroid belt between Mars and Jupiter. She is the brightest and the 3rd most massive asteroid after Ceres and Pallas. German astronomer, Heinrich Olbers, discovered Vesta about 10 hours after discovering Pallas. Vesta, the 4th asteroid discovered. Therefore, her asteroid number is 4.

Vesta orbits the Sun every 3.63 years and is retrograde three or four times during that period. Her shape is irregular, and she has many dark and light spots. In some ways, she is more of a protoplanet than an asteroid. She shows signs of volcanic activity and numerous craters from asteroid impacts. On her southern pole lies Rhea Silvia, the second largest volcano in our solar system (Olympus Mons on Mars is the first).

If we look at the chart at the time of Vesta's discovery, we find that Vesta was retrograde at 29 degrees Virgo when discovered, the anaretic degree of the sign that rules her. Uranus retrograde is near the ascendant, at 29 degrees Libra, and in opposition to Venus at 0 degrees Taurus, near the descendant.

There is a wide stellium in the 1st house in Scorpio; all are retrograde. If we were reading the chart of a woman, Vesta would be a powerful one! Discovered at the beginning of the Aries season on March 29th, 1807, the Sun at 5 degrees Aries is conjunct Hygiea at 7 degrees. Mercury, Nessus, and Quaoar are also there in her 6th temple. She is a healer, often dealing with abuse. Mercury opposite Uranus on her Ascendant indicates that she communicates with the universe or her higher self to assist in her healing work. Uranus is opposite Venus and semi-sextile Vesta (inconjunct Venus); freedom comes with unleashing attachment. Her service requires renunciation. She will learn that they are one and the same, that sexual liberation is freedom.

Vesta was present in the 11th temple at the time of discovery by Heinrich Wilhelm Olbers, and Chiron is at 3 degrees Aquarius, conjunct the IC at 5 degrees Aquarius. Wounded in her young environment, she heals from her root(s).

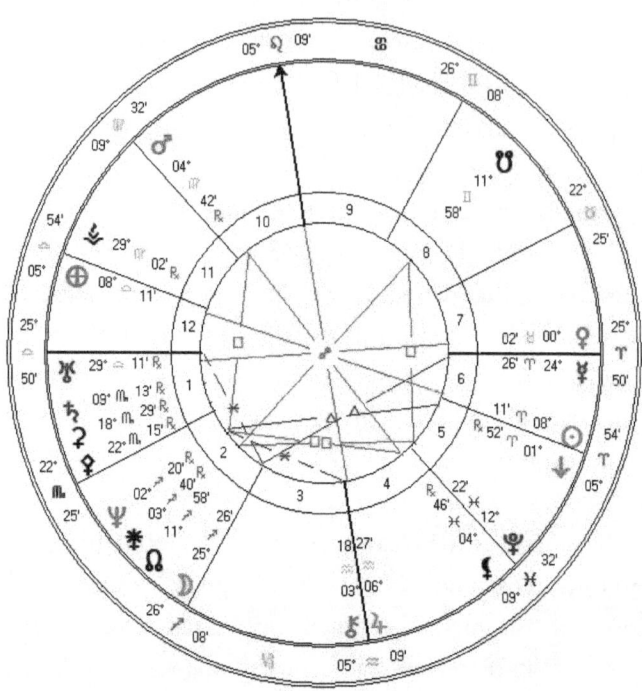

Jupiter/Chiron on the IC sextile Juno shows her contract or arrangement with her brother Zeus. Mercury is trining her Moon; she communicates her emotions readily for the highest good of all. Her moon is conjunct the Galactic Center, so her emotional foundation is freedom and truth.

Vesta entered her brother's home (3rd temple) and became domestic (4th temple). The 4th temple also represents the parents (Vesta was hurt by her father and then lived with her brother, Jupiter). Vesta may have cared for her niece, Pallas, as they are friends in myth. Ceres and Pallas are near conjunction in Scorpio in the 1st temple and loosely sextile Vesta in the 11th temple.

With a Libra Ascendant, we see it may be hard for her to make decisions, but it is the quality of decisions made that determines one's success. Many modern Vestals may find it is easier to give up responsibility and rely on the hierarchy to make decisions for them. Hence, the Will of God/Goddess is their Will.

Uranus on the Ascendant opposing Venus on the Descendant show that Vesta must have freedom in her relationships. She seeks an unusual type of love. She is devoted as long as there is free will in that devotion. She wants fidelity without the constant exchange, although she herself can become attached. Her partners and adversaries enjoy her unpredictable nature.

Vesta is involved in politics; Mars is retrograde in Virgo in the 10th temple. The discovery chart shows Vesta as highly critical and inwardly tenacious. She speaks for all, representing the people and the state. Vesta calls attention to the issues that need to be petrified, purified, or perished. She is influential and wields some power.

Many people with prominent Vesta are activists of some kind who work for the betterment of society and the state. Knowledge, desire to serve, and education are significant to anyone in this role. Vesta types are the timekeepers of history, keeping records and vital documents trusted upon them. They are also the keeper of secrets. Allowing them to be shared when the time is right is also a Vesta trait.

Vesta and the Physical World

I've read that the oldest goddess religions centered around the worship of trees. Many myths and legends mention the goddess transforming into a tree or plant (often to escape man, beast, or god). Tree worship is worldwide as trees provide food, shelter, and fuel for the fire. The goddess is the whole, three parts of the Tree of Life.

Biologically, Vesta was a nymph in one of her myths, a forest creature, transformed into one with the forest, a lotus tree. She ate from the trees, and they provide much-needed nourishment to sustain her fire: seeds, nuts, fruit, berries, spices, meat (from the animals in the forest). A hunter/gatherer diet is her nature.

Ecologically Vesta, as the Lotus tree, is a cooling force. Trees provide life-giving oxygen. We need that cooling force to balance the egoistic inferno. Fires also require oxygen to live. A tree provides shade, and volcanoes are known to cool the skies by blocking out the Sun through smoke and ash.

Vesta is part of the soil and the toxicity or fertility of the medium. Vesta, as a tree, also works with the soil systems, providing nutrients for other species. Trees add nutrients and biology to the soil and surrounding environment; the most fertile soils are those of the forests and near old trees. When a tree dies in the woods it is not wasted; it becomes food or fuel for all the living beings in its community and habitat. All of Earth's systems are connected. Society cannot change one system without also altering all other systems. Vesta is about providing a safe, satisfying, sacred home.

Vesta is also the fire within. When a volcano erupts, the magma is released and the ash becomes fertile soil after working with the earth cycles. Forest fires burn the dead wood, allowing new growth to thrive. Fire and water cleanse and purify the world. Like using compost, biochar, sand, or clay as soil amendments, Vesta works the soil for renewal and growth.

Fire is a living, breathing being which forges, sustains, and destroys. Like humans, fire breathes oxygen and excretes carbon dioxide and other gases. Vesta is present in birth, life, and death, and she has links to the trees and the life cycles of the soil and forests. Most "fuel" for fire is composed of three elements; carbon, hydrogen, and oxygen. Burning them in the presence of oxygen produces carbon dioxide and water with some carbon monoxide. The ashes from fire contain many oxides: calcium, sodium, potassium, and other minerals and metals. Learning this process and the chemicals composed is another important lesson to a Vestal—similar to alchemy or the glaze process of pottery.

> *It is nearly a week away from the July 4th Lunar Eclipse 2020. We are experiencing dust in the air and pollution caused by ourselves. Not taking care of the soil/Earth has taken a toll. Vesta is conjunct the Sun exactly (within three minutes).*

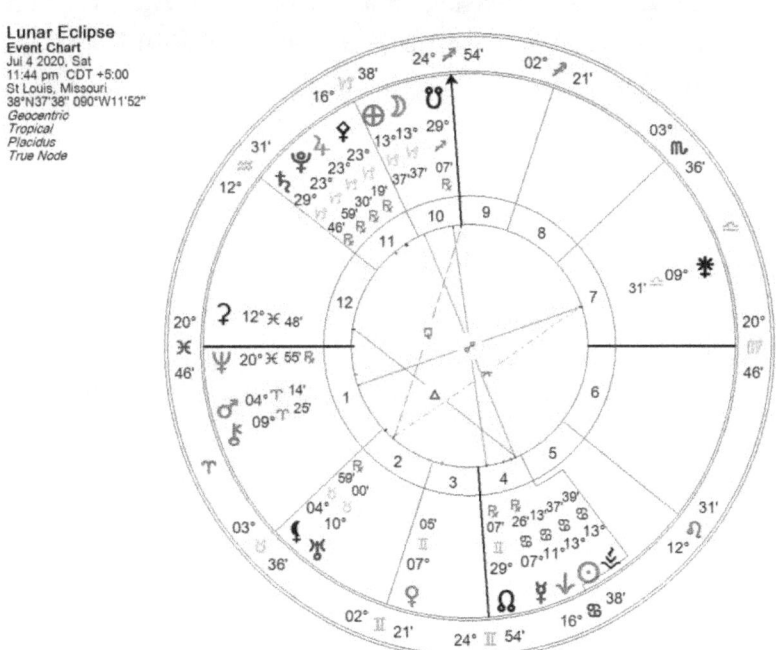

Vesta rules ecology, and her asteroid has been prominent in many Earthly events. Due to her presence and her influence, many heritage sites have been established. For transits, Vesta represents times of transition. She is prominent this year, 2020, as it is a time of transition for everyone on Earth! It is my understanding that people in power are finally starting to do something about human-inducing climate change. Vesta in Virgo is square the nodes the first half of 2021.

Vesta is the fire of the Earth, and we know that we must divest from oil due to its high volatility in causing climate change[8] through its extraction, distribution, consumption, and waste. Everything we have done in the past is measured in the soil. Soil quality influences so many other things. It is our Earth. We rely on the Earth for food. The quality of soil provides security for now and the future of food. Ceres represents the seasons of food, and Vesta is the political voice.

The International Union of Soil Scientists proclaimed 2015-2024 the International Decade of Soils. The International Year of the Soil, 2015, determined by the United Nations at the 68th session on December 20th, 2013. December 5th is World Soil Day. The Sabian symbol for that day (Sun at about 13 degrees Sagittarius) is *A Widow's Past is Brought to Light*.

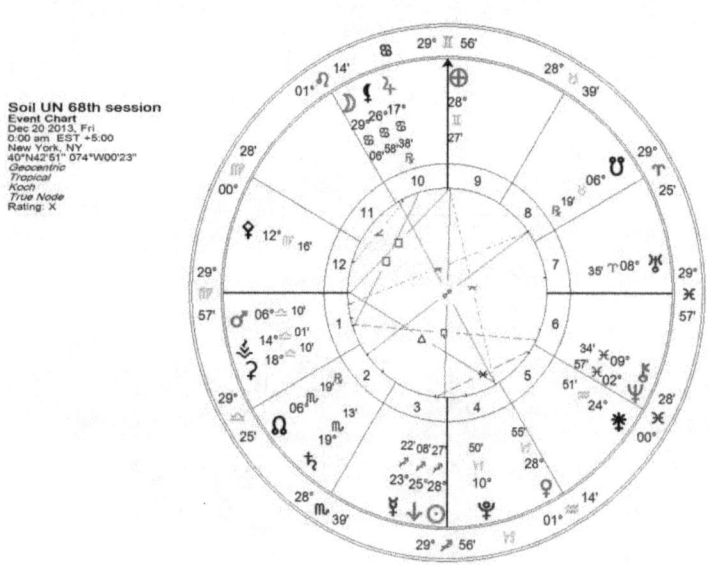

---

[8] https://paulbeckwith.net/2020/06/22/jet-stream-configurations-consequences-of-abrupt-climate-change/

Vesta was conjunct Ceres in Virgo since the UN began their assembly in September of 2013. Not far away, Mars is semi-sextile the North Node. The Sun is on the IC in connection with the root! 2015 was the Year of the Soil and the "four blood-moon eclipses". According to the solar eclipse chart, in March 2015, Vesta was conjunct the Ascendant and semi-sextile the eclipse. Vesta is very prominent in this year's (2020) eclipses also.

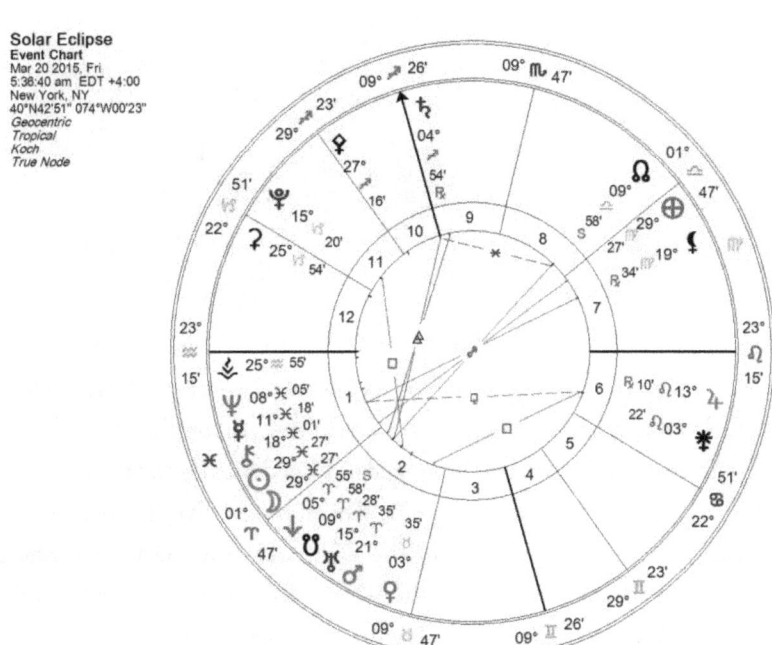

In the chart for the next eclipse during the solar month of Aries, Vesta is conjunct Neptune in Pisces and sextile Mars (Aries energy) in Taurus. Earth and fire are huge influences in this chart. Volcano Calbuco erupted in Southern Chile that month.

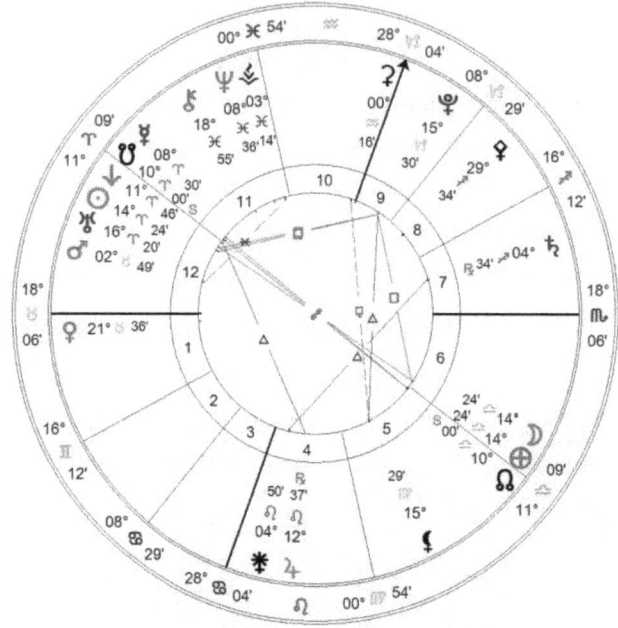

During the summer of 2015, a new bill (The DARK Act) was set up, after the Monsanto Protection Act of 2013, part of a farm bill in the U.S. that allowed Monsanto to continue to profit even if their products become linked to carcinogens. This denied citizens the "right to know".[9] Mike Pompeo (former R-KS representative, Monsanto and Koch Brothers supporter, head of the CIA, and now the United States Secretary of State), amended the law (H.R. 1599) on genetically engineered(GE) food labeling. It not only prohibits all labeling of GMOs (genetically modified organisms) but made it unlawful for states or local governments to restrict GMO crops in any way.

Vesta was a baby at one degree Aries, conjunct the nadir or Imum Coeli (the I.C. is the hidden or least conscious part of the chart) when the Dark Act became printed. Pallas in the first house, planning and

---

[9] https://www.centerforfoodsafety.org/press-releases/3961/the-monsanto-protection-act-is-back-and-worse-than-ever

strategy, opposes Mars/Sun, the purpose of war, action, accidents in the 7th temple of partnerships and open enemies, in a T-square with Chiron the wounded healer, in the 3rd temple of local publications of Pisces substance, a poisonous arrow. Ceres Rx in Aquarius opposes Venus. The nodes are prominent and stationed. Mercury was also stationed in Gemini, 6th temple.

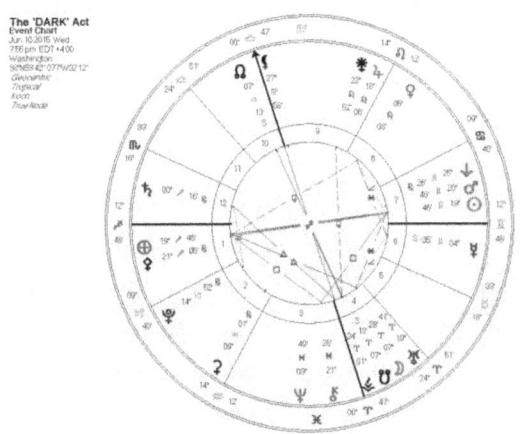

The eclipses in September of 2015 were also very Vesta prominent. The Partial Solar Eclipse on the 13th has Vesta on the Midheaven. This one was only visible to Southern Africa and Antarctica. Vesta in Aries intensifies focus.

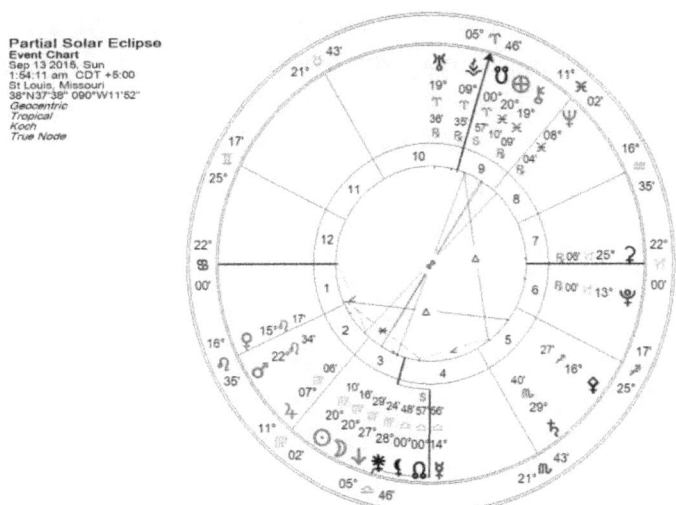

A new human-like species, Homo Naledi, was found by female archaeologist Dr. Debra Bolter deep inside the South African Rising Star cave system in the Bloubank River valley near the Cradle of Humankind World Heritage Site. The small passageway took a group of tiny, Vestal-like women to excavate. The discovery became news on September 10th, 2015, three days before the solar eclipse.

The Total Lunar Eclipse on September 27th/28th made a conjunction to Vesta and an inconjunction to Mars. The eclipse was visible to half of the world; its shadow stretched from Greenland and Antarctica.

A breakdown of events during September 2015 includes the worldwide migrant crisis caused by climate change, war, and depletion of natural resources, as well as massive forest fires in California. United States President Barack Obama was the first U.S. President to visit the Arctic circle in Alaska to witness climate change/global warming and the devastation of oil drilling for himself.

The Pope was on tour and had many international meetings around the world, including being the first pope to address the United States Congress. On September 24th, 2015, he gave a speech on family, unity, and our need to take care of all in the face of the changing world. Chinese president Xi Jinxing visited the U.S. for the first time.[10] It concerned the state, and he met with the leaders of Microsoft and Boeing in Seattle before going to Washington D.C. on the 25th.

Other events included a Neolithic "super-henge" discovery at Durrington Walls under three feet of Earth, an enormous 8.3 earthquake that rocked Chile, and the US NOAA (United States National Oceanic Atmospheric Administration) recorded the hottest summer ever in the Northern Hemisphere, topped by by 2016 and 2019. Indonesia's air pollution was the worst ever due to deliberately lit

---

[10] https://obamawhitehouse.archives.gov/the-press-office/2015/09/25/fact-sheet-president-xi-jinpings-state-visit-united-states

forest fires to clear land for agriculture. Scientists revealed that over three million people a year die from air pollution alone, and also discussed the discovery of flowing water on Mars.

Giant holes in Siberia have been bursting open in the Earth—likely methane gas explosions due to the nearby oil and gas production fields. The first Siberian hole discovery happened on September 27th, 2013. I do not have an exact time for this, but Vesta began in late Leo following Ceres into Virgo in a close conjunction all month. Vesta/Ceres was in an Earth Grand Trine with Pluto and the South Node. Vesta was sextile North Node/Saturn, trine Neptune/Chiron, and trine Uranus. The volcano aspect points to the Aries Point chart's ascendant (MC at midnight).

More holes have recently appeared—Siberia is apparently full of methane hills and pockets. When pressure builds and becomes too much, they explode. Another eclipse occurred on the 4th of July, 2020, the latest discovery of more methane scars. Vesta was conjunct the Sun in the 4th temple and trine Ceres in the 12th.

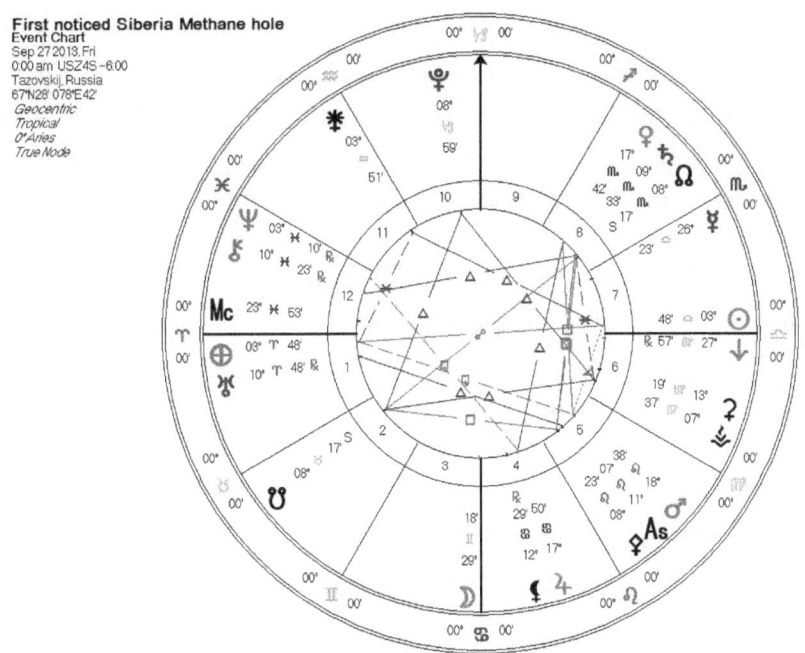

The more I study Vesta, the more I find her connection with Earthly fumes, explosions, and mind-altering space/substances. Studying nature has led me to believe Vesta presents with volcanoes. She is prominent in the astrology charts but not always in the aspect pattern of volcanoes. Vesta is the stuff of the Earth that escapes the volcano. She is the smoke, the gases, the ash, the fire, the liquid magma from within. Essentially, Vesta is the fuel of the Earth. From trees, to gas, to oil, to geothermal, she is energy—and the sacredness of energy. She constricts and concentrates fuel for the highest possible good—duty to her home, Mother Earth.

Vesta also represents the home and its importance; staying home, working from home, learning from home, sustaining home. Bacchus, drunk on petroleum (oil) is stuck in greed and globalism.

Methane gas is a highly flammable and combustible asphyxiant. Exposure and symptoms can range from mild to severe--acute to long-term. When exposed, oxygen may be administered or external defibrillation or cardio-pulmonary resuscitation (from nevadanano.com). Breathing methane gas or oxygen-depleted air can lead to death by asphyxiation. High levels of methane reduce oxygen in the atmosphere. The effects of methane inhalation cause similar effects as imbuing alcohol: headaches, facial flushing, mood changes, and emotional responses, memory loss and decreased alertness, nausea, vomiting, weakness, fatigue, fainting, convulsions, etc. When severe, methane inhalation can cause changes in breathing which affects heart rate, possible vertigo, numbness, unconsciousness, to eventual death (https://assets.publishing.service.gov.uk). In 1981, companies like Exxon came to know about carbon dioxide increase from petroleum production, and became aware of their actions on the climate. They began to be concerned, and started to realize that the environment is existential for business and not just for the business or environmental sake. The long-term damage is ecocidal.

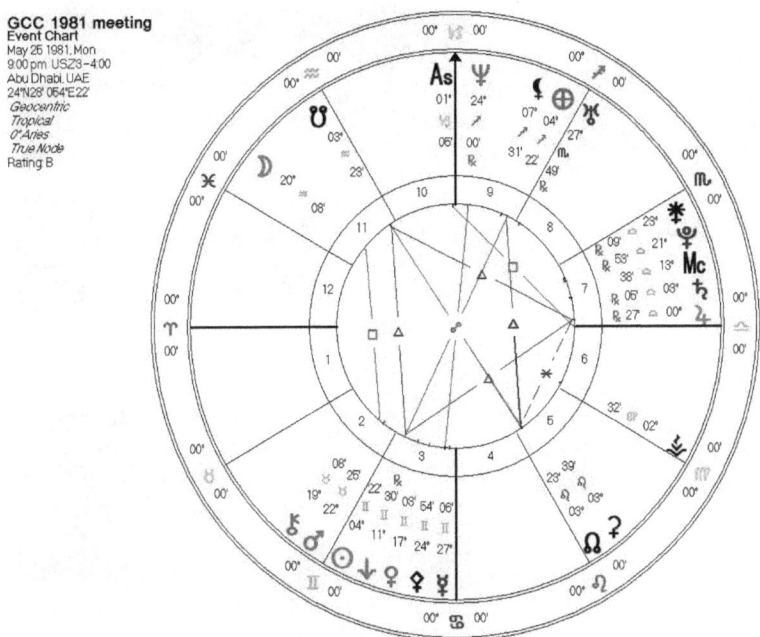

However, a group of wealthy oil tycoons formed a group called the Global Climate Coalition (GCC), hid the science, and opposed any regulations to mitigate climate change. In the chart of the first known GCC meeting (before they established the group in 1989), Vesta is at the midpoint of Ceres/North node Leo conjunction and retrograde Jupiter/Saturn conjunction in Libra (we experienced the Jupiter-Saturn conjunction in Aquarius this year, 2020, trine the same degree). Pluto/Juno conjunction is also retrograde in Libra. A hidden contract between kings of the world took place in the dark.

In 2010 a major explosion occurred on the BP oil rig, Deepwater Horizon, located in the Gulf of Mexico. It was an eye-opener! Many wanted to divest from oil after seeing the devastation it causes for the economy and environment, but, in an oil-based and corporate own society, that is no easy feat.

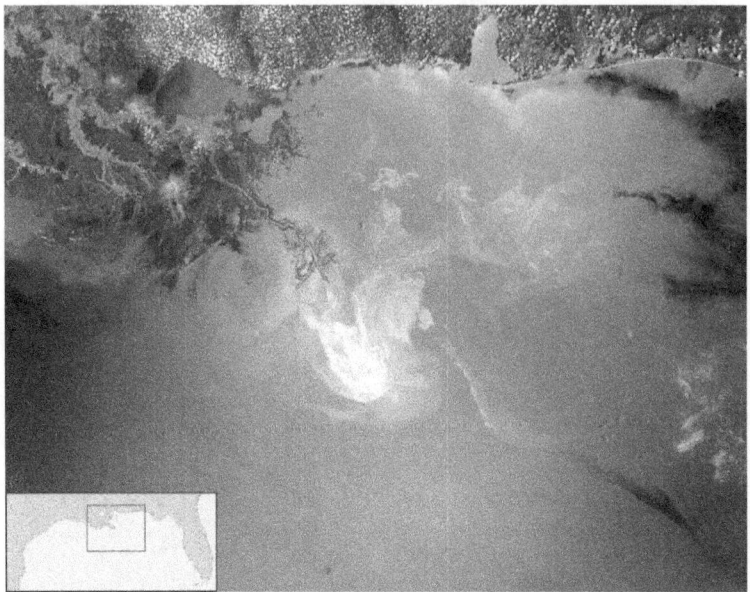

Figure 6: Aerial view of the massive BP oil spill 2010. NASA - NASA's Terra Satellites Sees Spill on May 24. http://nasa.gov.

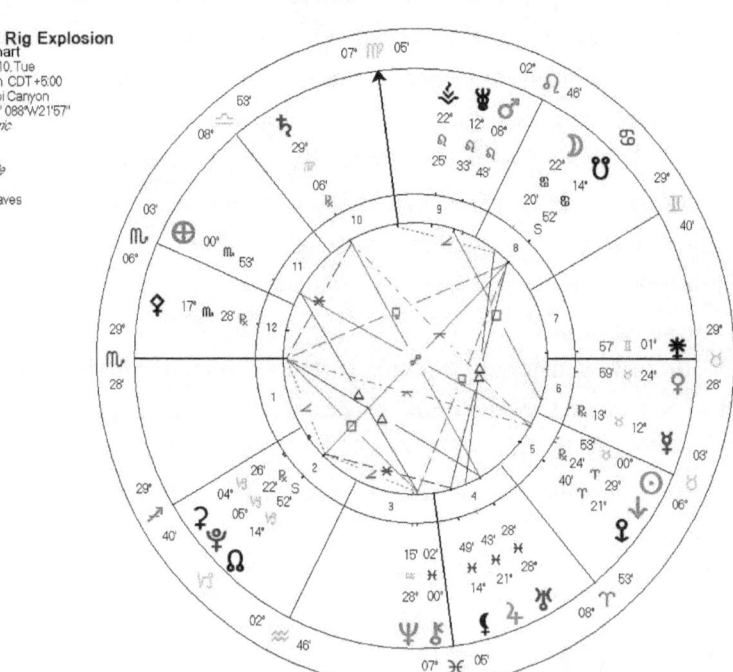

The damage was irrefutable and resulted in the loss of life, ecosystems, and businesses. They could not stop the flow of oil. An estimated five million barrels of oil escaped the Earth and into the ocean. Documented as sealed in September of 2010, the spot was still found to be leaking in 2012.

In the chart, Vesta is closest to the Midheaven in a fire sign. There is a Grand Trine in water, with Uranus in Pisces opposed retrograde Saturn (conjunct Vesta in the Vesta discovery chart). Ceres is conjunct retrograde Pluto and opposes the moon. Mercury was also retrograde, square Mars, and in aspect to the Nodes. The Vulcan/Sun conjunction is in a Yod with Saturn and Ascendant. Chiron/Neptune is conjunct on the IC and sextile the Sun.

In December of 2019, the United Nations met, yet again, to discuss richer developed countries paying to keep forests intact in undeveloped countries. The meeting should have taken place in China, but the pandemic began. The meeting took place in Rome, Italy 17th-19th of December.[11] China attended virtually. Vesta, in the sign of values, is trine Ceres in Capricorn.

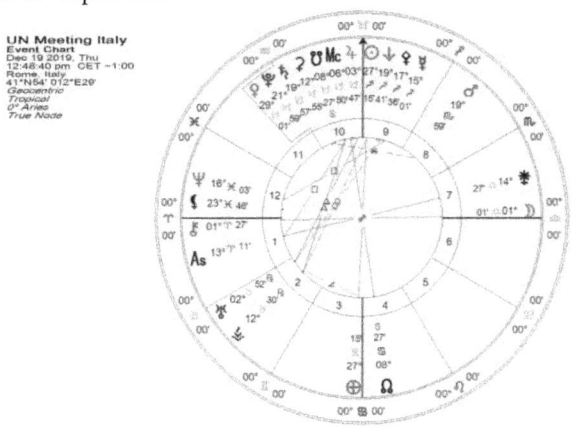

---

[11] https://www.worldheritage.org
Italy | Meetings Coverage and Press Releases - United Nations *https://www.un.org/press/en/country/italy*. United Nations Secretary-General António Guterres travelled from Geneva, to Rome, on Tuesday evening, 17 December 2019.

This year, 2020, has been a Vesta-prominent year! People have been forced into their homes by the pandemic and the change of ecology, a hidden issue that has powered many changes. It is time to make or recreate our sacred space(s). Hestia, the homemaker, is busy, busy! I have had little time this year to work on much else. This "caretaker" goddess deserves attention again. Appreciate the cook, artist, caretaker, nurse or nanny, provider of desires, etc., before and after the "meal"!

2020 has also been a year of other goddess planets/asteroids prominent and becoming more independent. They have had to take on more than their share of the work of motivating people to go their own way. That is part of Vesta's energy. She can only be a caretaker of someone for so long before she has others or herself to care for.

> *"The greatest of teachers won't hesitate to leave you there by yourself..."* -Live; I Alone.

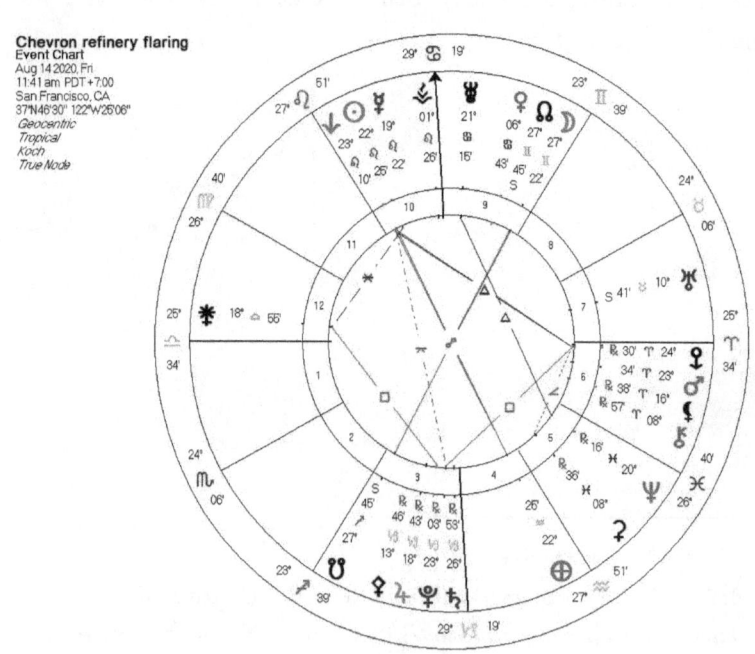

On August 14, 2020, the Chevron refinery in North Richmond California, sent flares up from the factory.[12] Billows of toxic, black smoke filled the air, creating a bit of fear from the locals as they had just passed the eighth anniversary of the same Chevron flares that sent 15,000 people to the hospital (Vesta was conjunct Jupiter in Gemini and Hygiea was in a T-square with the Nodes).

Volcanoes

Volcanic eruptions could have sparked the worship of Vesta as a deity. One of the most significant natural events in Roman history was the eruption of Mount Vesuvius, long after the height of the Vesta cult. Pompeii became ruins when Mount Vesuvius erupted on August 24, 79 CE., and there is a Volcano Aspect in the chart. A Volcano Aspect is four objects, two trines connected by a square with a semi-sextile or opening on the opposite end. Saturn retrograde in Aquarius, trine Jupiter in Gemini, Jupiter square the Sun and Mercury in Virgo, and trine the moon in Capricorn. The opening is pointed at the 5th temple of sex for fun; Saturn is semi-sextile the moon. Ceres and Venus are at the midpoint of the square. Vesta is leading a stellium. A mutable grand cross is also in the picture.

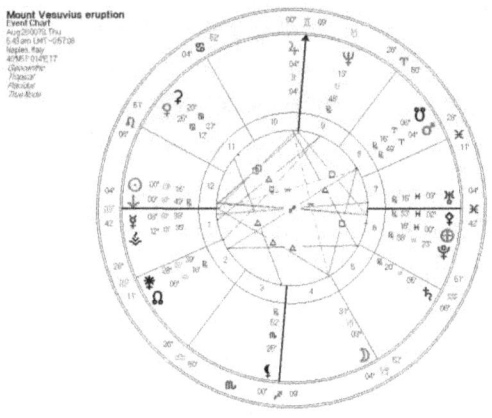

---

[12] https://richmondpulse.org/2020/08/19/chevron-is-on-fire-again-change-is-long-overdue/

I recently visited an expedition of Pompeii and saw a room specifically dedicated to highly erotic murals and paintings from Roman brothels. These paintings served as scenes for fetish preference, stimulation, or instruction. Pompeii remains sheathed in layers of magma and volcanic ash almost 82 feet (25 meters) deep. The scene is very macabre; the Pompeii inhabitants and their stories lie trapped in time. Still, the bodies of the deceased lie hardened in their funeral shroud, forever entombed in the aftermath of Mount Vesuvius.

In the Virgo new moon chart of 2019, there was a volcano pattern; the Sun/Moon was trine Uranus in Taurus and square Ceres in Sagittarius, and Ceres was trine Chiron in Aries. Vesta was hanging out closest to the Midheaven at 26 degrees Taurus and square the Leo ascendant. Vesta seems to play very prominent roles when placed on the Midheaven.

The Virgo new moon chart for 2019 also has a mutable grand cross! The moon was square the stellium with Vesta. The top or opening of the Volcano Aspect position is in the Eastern part of the chart. Stromboli in Italy had a tremendous second eruption about two days before the new moon. Popocatepetl, another stratovolcano, erupted, and hurricane Dorian began near this time. I thought Dorian was a strange hurricane because it seemed to appear over the Virgin Islands and Grenada—the same place Kick'em Jenny, an immense underwater volcano, is located. A video of the storm surge in nearby Guadalupe was incredible. Water rushed in from the ocean more than it fell out of the sky! Scientists concur that a Kick'em Jenny eruption would spark a tsunami. The fast-warming waters creating warmer air above spark the potential to form a hurricane, such as Hurricane Dorian.

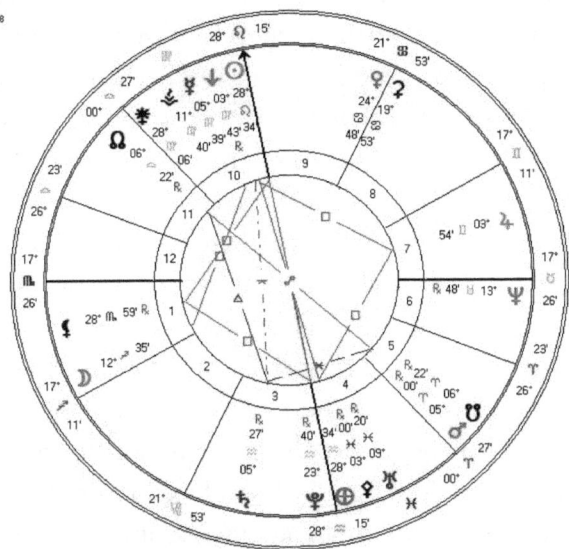

Mount Vesuvius Eruption
Natal Chart
Aug 24 0079, Tue
12:00 pm LMT -0:57:08
Naples, Italy
40°N51' 014°E17'
Geocentric
Tropical
Placidus
True Node

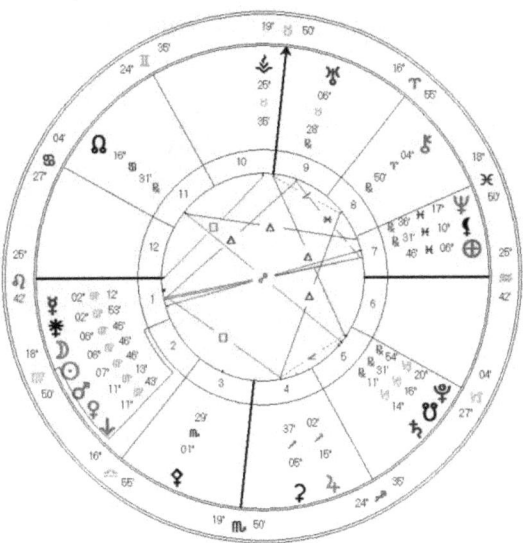

Virgo new moon 2019
Event Chart
Aug 30 2019, Fri
6:37 am CDT +6:00
St Louis, Missouri
38°N37'36" 090°W11'52"
Geocentric
Tropical
Placidus
True Node

On August 4th, 2020, hurricane Isaias tore up the Northeast coast of the U.S. I was watching the clock/astrology chart and noticed familiar patterns of natural disasters. (The chart I pulled was for 3:04 pm, New York City.) The volcano aspect points to the first house. Tornadoes formed on land caused by the hurricane on the Northeast coast. Vesta is closely involved in the volcano pattern.

In Beirut, Lebanon, a warehouse caught on fire, and then an explosion occurred, sending a mushroom cloud up and a shock wave out throughout the city. Buildings became leveled on the port, and windows were blown out all over the city. Massive rainstorms in China cause extreme flooding on the Yangtze River, and on August 5th, a fire broke out at 6:30 pm in the United Arab Emirates' new industrial area in Ajman, 50 km away from Dubai. The chart for Dubai is very similar to Beirut. Many other storms and fires occurred around the globe that week, including a gas station explosion in Russia. A square between Juno and Pallas in Capricorn (stellium): a tough deal or one gone bad, with a Jupiter/Mars square as a possible indication of war.

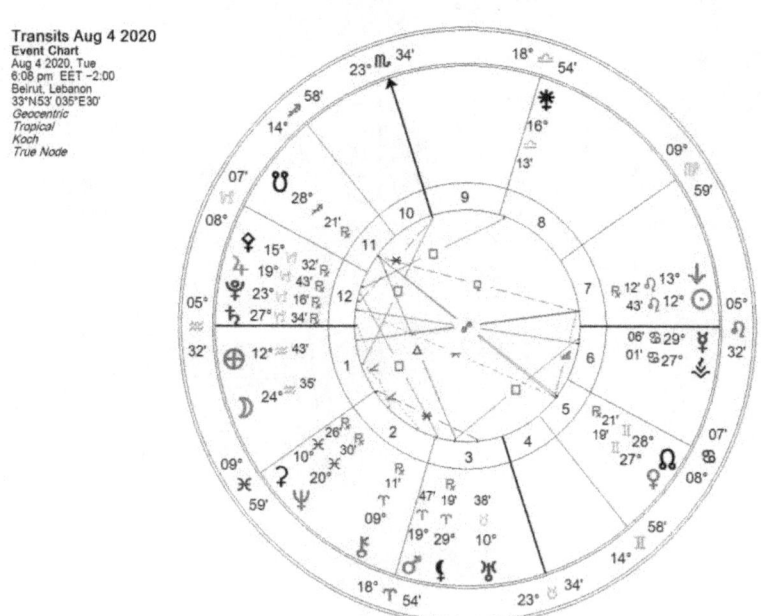

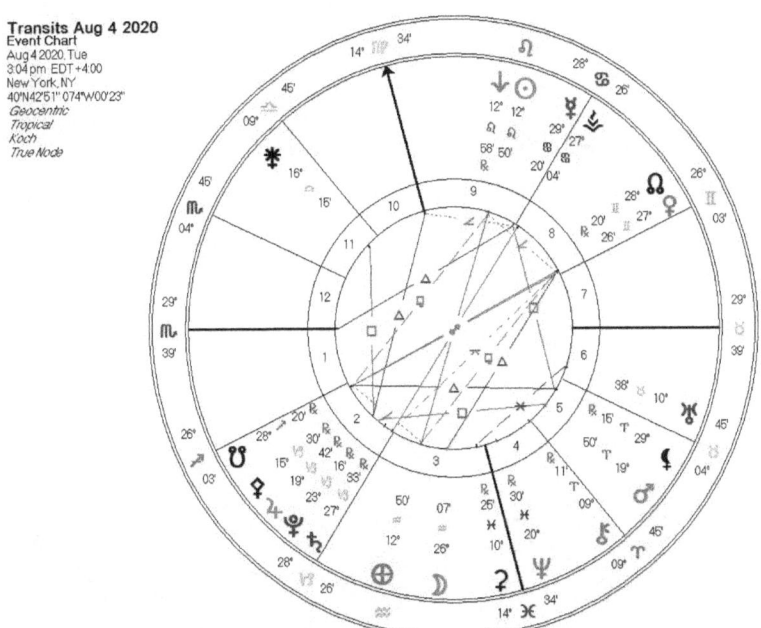

The Jupiter/Saturn conjunction in Aquarius, 2020.

Vesta in Virgo was opposite Neptune and the Moon in Pisces, and square the lunar nodes during the Jupiter/Saturn conjunction December 21, 2020. A possible representation of a deception and sacrifice to the gods, Jupiter/Saturn coming together is like the Gods of the gods coming together.

Ceres and Nessus (10-11 degrees) were also in Pisces. Neptune has a way of making everything seem surreal, drunk, or dreamy; the 12th temple fogs reality! It is in this temple where hidden things take place undercover. With Vesta in the 6th temple, in the Aries Point Chart, the focus is on work and health institutions, especially hidden governments (12th temple).

The biggest news on that day was the European Union Pfizer deal: emergency release or Conditional Market Authorisation (CMA) of an experimental, mRNA(genetically modified) vaccine—and a massive Russian hack of American government agencies. In the chart, Vesta is the handle of a bucket pattern.

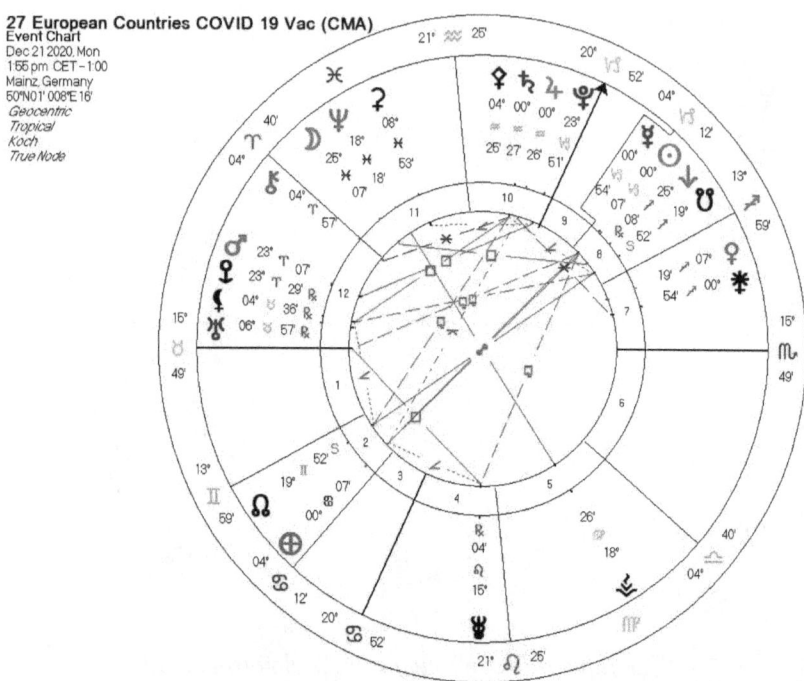

The chart is nine minutes before the press release of the Pfizer/EU deal. The Sun/Mercury conjunction, in the 8th temple, is sesquisquare Hygiea (at the bottom) and the Ascendant. The Sun/Mercury conjunction is the midpoint between Juno and the Jupiter/Saturn conjunction. Hygiea is square the ascendant at 15 degrees of fixed signs.

The 15-degree points of the four fixed signs, Taurus, Leo, Scorpio, or Aquarius are called the Avatar Degree or The Gates of the Avatars. They are the midpoint between the solstices and equinoxes. It is considered a magical point where the impossible finds a way. Both Ascendant and Hygiea are in a sesquiquadrate, better known as a sesquisquare, to the Sun/Mercury conjunction. Hygiea is quindecile the Jupiter/Saturn conjunction. Although these are minor aspects, the sesquiquadrates and quindecilee are exact (within one degree)! There are two more sesquiquadrates involving the nodes, BML, and Pallas. The lunar nodes are stationed, representing a moon wobble: instabilities with possible catastrophic events.

A sesquisquadrate is an angle of 135 degrees that causes irritation between the plants in aspect, and action may be required to resolve the conflict between them. A quindecile is an angle of 165 degrees between two points or planets. With a quindecile involved, there is obsession that causes disruption and/or determined motivation between the two planets.

The Mars/Pluto square suggests forceful domination used in a dangerous way. Mars, the planet of war, may also represent sickness and Pluto, death or hidden awareness. The sextile between the Jupiter/Saturn conjunction and Juno may represent a contract between big shots (no pun intended). This aspect makes a Yod to the Earth. Something cynical occurred due to a focus of the Earth.

Part 3
Mystery and Mirroring

More Secrets of Vesta

Vesta is the first and the last—the first to be born and consumed and the last to be ejected and born-again. She is the burning, yearning, passion of desire that refuses to be penetrated by others and surrenders to the universal highest Will.

Vesta puts others' needs before her own, and she also often puts her work before her own needs. Spiritual beings even put off their spiritual studies and practice for their sacred work, which is often spiritual service to others. Relationships share feedback, like birds in song echoing each other on the breeze. She inspires the firelight in others. Without it, there is no life.

I have come across a few polyamorous and a couple of transgender people during this journey. Not all of a person's needs will be satiated by loving, or even being, one person. The people I have met who are polyamorous seem to be more loving individuals who understand love cannot be contained, sex is for everyone, and all are creatures of the universe. The open relationships of the polyamorous seem to suggest that a relationship does not have to end for another to begin; they simply change or evolve when needed.

A Vestal is devoted to her cause and her life; she is very much a part of her community. I believe that throughout the ages, Vestal types who allowed themselves to have sex might typically fall into a category of polyamory. Certainly they can have had only one partner; however, it would have been a rare case, as Vestals were devoted to their community. It was easy to develop a relationship with self, but to be devoted to an Empire, one must form many relationships with many different people.

In a way, I think of Ceres, the mother who loves unconditionally. I do not think everyone can be polyamorous. I think it is something evolutionary, even if devoid of sex. Of course, some use it as an excuse to have sex with whoever they want—this is also true, but an evolved soul understands the connection she shares with all that inhabit the Earth. To take a vow is to limit oneself.

In the Christian Bible, there is a passage that says not to take any oaths, and there is a good reason behind it. Although many nuns today still take many different vows (usually chastity, obedience, and poverty), they understand that they can break them, intentionally or not, or the oath can outlive its purpose.

Vestals were a part of Rome's politics, and part of politics today as well. If she feels the need to speak up and say what must be said, then it is her duty and right to do so. Vows are easily broken. Even nuns know and recognize this as we are all merely human.

Vesta putting the needs of others before her own often leads to the downfall of sacred vows. Oaths have a way of burdening us. Sure, they are paramount or meaningful at the time and can even be protective, but when severed, they can lead to guilt or shaming. In the more puritan era of Rome, breaking vows resulted in the common shaming of others. For some, they were the cause or reason of death.

We know today that guilt and shame are like poison and should be avoided or overcome. I knew shame from a loved one's actions and the experience was excruciating. I wanted to die, be tied, bound and whipped, or become a nun living in the safety of the sanctuary. The shamed were stoned, buried alive, or whipped for making a mistake. Vestals are nuns devoted to a life of solitude, service, and community, and they may punish themselves when mistakes occur.

> *I craved my solitude and still do. I need to be of service to others, but at the same time I choose to share with the larger community. When I broke my chastity vow, I did not feel shame because I broke it with my husband, although, I did feel a little pained. I gave up my work as my most important focus. My sacred work became put on hold, and my focus shifted to family obligations.*

Vesta, in her negative stance, is an escapist. One who chooses the path of a Vestal is, usually one that desires to escape the mundane life of marriage and child-rearing. To die is to exit as a martyr, to be bound and whipped is to arrive as the victim, and to become a nun is to disappear into solitude, religion, or spiritual addiction. These are all forms of escape. But as long as one lives, one must deal with life, death, and all things in between.

A Vestal type must learn what her triggers are, must come to know her strengths and weaknesses. Some things she must keep secret; she cannot put herself in a trap. This knowledge takes time; one must get to know one's self. Learning who one is spiritually and sexually, the light and the shadow side of the personality, are essential. Once we know and understand our traps and triggers, we will learn how to guard ourselves. When we know who we are, we know our purpose and where to put our focus.

Vesta needs to be comfortable with death, for in death, there is power. Sometimes when a loved one dies, it focuses us. Organizations get started, a "search for the cure" begins, a study to understand the "why" of the situation commences, as might lawsuits, protests, awareness—change in general occurs because of death. Death often inspires the desire to live for a higher purpose and selfless love. Vesta teaches these things.

Death also teaches us to let go. A silly example but a good one: I was working one day in the pottery studio. A woman who had been there all day had all of her pots on one board. When she got up to put her work on the shelf, the board broke, and every single piece of pottery shattered on the floor. She stood completely still, devastated—all that time and effort she had put in turned to dust. Letting go is a lesson every potter learns, so it is therefore not a complete loss or waste of time. She can still keep the practice she has performed in advancing her skill and her experience of creating and destroying. Perhaps that is a Ceres lesson—letting go of what we made in our image.

A healthy Vesta has come to terms with her shadow. She can focus on what she wants and knows what she loves. Vesta is our urge for what matters, setting things right when they get turned upside-down.

Vesta keeps her focus on the mission and service. She has an inner union, having gone through the alchemical process of shedding the dross to reveal the gold or the diamond. Her goal is mastery of the soul and higher spiritual union; she grabs you in a trance, like a moth to a flame. Vesta has certainty in her craft and chosen path. She is that moment when everything comes into focus, reveals where we are and what we need, and instantly knows what we have to do. She sets her intention and follows through with a steady practice.

The keeper of the fire is responsible for keeping it contained. A Vestal steadies the fire and keeps the flame ablaze, tending to love, honor, and sacrifice. She lets it burn, contained in the hearth, and watches over it. What we cherish is sacred to Vesta.

Desires change, as do we. The goddess is a healer of sexual dysfunction. Priapus suffered from permanent engorgement of the penis until intercourse, and then suffered impotence. The story of Vesta and Priapus appears to be lacking some important point. Both gods descended from heaven to the hillside to preside, and both were beholden to the Earth. The sacred phallus that appears in her flame may have been his; the origins are ambiguous. She may have removed it from Priapus to relieve his suffering. Vesta is very kind; she could have thrown it into her sacred fire. Since he is a god, it would have survived. By doing so, perhaps Vesta cured Priapus from his curse. Her holy fire could also represent her ovulating womb in which she became the virgin mother.

The virgin and whore are two steps or stages of the Vestal. They can blend or are experienced at different points in a Vestal's life. Both are creative and destructive; too much sex can be just as dangerous as not enough. Individual sexuality is sacred, and there is always an initiation or a critical self-examination. She can flip-flop on a dime or stay one way for lengthy periods. Vesta is about the decisions around sharing or not sharing one's sacred space.

Vestals represent the young women who stayed in the camp or home to keep the fire going while the others were away, protecting the camp and hosting new arrivals. She is a vessel holding space for others, including those not in their bodies. A purgatory for a new life, a Vestal becomes a mother one way or another. The last ten years spent as a

Vestal Virgin was similar to a Mother Superior in a monastery or the Veiled Isis, teaching and instructing the young.

Vesta types may be taken for granted. It is important that they receive the proper training, in order to understand the secrets and withstand causing injury to themselves. A person with Vesta prominent may experience the controversy between the virgin and the sacred prostitute, regardless of gender.

Standing firm in her willpower and not faltering to become like the other, Vesta avoids failure. She has a sixth sense and knows what others need. When aware of their intentions, there is a choice to hide away and retreat to her own sacred space or give them what they desire. Vesta in Scorpio adheres to Eros and Thanatos, or love and death. To psychologist Sigmund Freud, love and death are what drive people in life. Either connection or complete dissolution is what one craves. Vesta is the goddess of devotion. In Scorpio, she is all or nothing.

Vesta gives her initiates confidence and ignites our power within. She sees the potential in all and feeds their fire so they may have the confidence to become their highest self. Sometimes the initiate becomes so concentrated on the guru or Vestal that they may lose focus of the real purpose. This is when Vesta or the Vestal must step back and withdraw from these distractions.

Vesta is not to be possessed. If attempted, she may cut them off. If a Vestal decides to enter into a relationship, it is for a higher purpose. She seeks the divine, and if she finds the divine within a relationship, she will be devoted to one—although she will still need to acquire her alone time on occasion, as a romantic relationship often overwhelms the senses and hinders other forms of relating that can benefit us.

Psychology/Biology and Vesta

> *"One thorn of experience is worth a whole wilderness of warning."* -James Russell Lowell

Vesta, linked to Virgo, is biological. Vesta, linked to Scorpio, is psychological. When it comes to sex, the two are one. Sex is an organic act that affects the psyche. Vesta knows how to transmute orgasm and sexual creativity. Sex creates babies and higher spiritual states. Through transmutation, conception happens without the physical act of sex.

Often, where Vesta is concerned, one does not allow oneself to have sex. Sometimes something has happened where we are not allowed to express our sexuality with another. Influences that block sexual expression include: bonds, vows, marriage, STDs, confinement, fear of punishment, guilt, uncleanliness, bodily shame, involuntary celibacy, lack of self-discipline, or a history of abuse.

Vesta's view around sex is nontraditional. She does not, per se, want to engage in a committed partnership for sex; instead, she uses sex for healing. Vesta's focus is always devotional. True love is free from attachment and can erupt in orgasmic intensity. The type of sex Vesta may crave can be anything from body screaming to mellow fluidity to meditative yoga that resembles the transformative dance of the cosmos (Shiva/Shakti).

People often look to others to fulfill them. In extreme cases, looking for desire-fulfillment in others causes issues on a physical, emotional, and psychological level. Families can also mess up our lives, especially in a society such as ancient Rome—or our own. In the time of purity, any woman that had nonmarital sex or whom anyone considered "unclean" was cast off as a non-citizen of Rome. All family secrets were kept in order to avoid being ostracized. Perhaps this is one of the reasons Vestals were chosen so young, although another reason may be to spiritualize the self/child to connect spiritually with others when one is mature enough to have such relations.

What we receive from others who care about us and how they respond to our vulnerabilities can diminish our need for sexual misconduct or material things, however. Listening to the body is the most natural way to trust yourself. Courage and self-awareness are essential. Introspection and sharing with others allow us to understand that we are all human. We are not alone in our experiences and desires, but we can be whole unto our own.

Sex is half of Vesta; it can be healing. The sacred phallus is there for deep penetration. Spiritual orgasm often causes the female to ejaculate. It is different than male ejaculation as it is pure white, thicker, and usually more abundant. Amrita is most sacred and divine liquid energy granted to those who invoke the goddess. Ejaculation is a gigantic physical release that causes the body to relax into complete bliss. It is not the only way to attain spiritual euphoria, but this state of bliss is often the reason sex is sought. There are many ways to bring this about; it is a process of getting to know the self and what turns on the self. It does require surrender—if you surrender to your bliss, you will experience it to its fullest.

You will have difficulty in dealing with sex if you are internally condemning it. For example, the Catholic Church was unprepared to take on sexual abuse in the church because of repression and condemnation indoctrination; to them, sex is a sin. This ideology has pushed the belief that sex should be sinful, therefore, exacerbating the problem. Sex is spiritual when treated within the proper context.

Sex can empower, and it can maim. It is one of the most powerful human abilities; through sex, we can reach higher levels of consciousness. A healthy sexuality is like a healthy ego; you feel powerful and in charge of yourself and your situation. It is another form of obedience, being true to oneself. One nun from the U.S. (Cheryl Reed in *Unveiled: the Hidden Lives of Nuns*), explained that her vow of obedience means obedience to herself alone. But one also needs to be present and aware of the spiritual, emotional, and physical essences of others, allowing obedience to natural laws.

Being humble and in wonder and admiration for nature are also traits of a healthy sexuality. Sex is spiritual, emotional, and physical.

Sex is the heal-all; however, if you have an issue spiritually, emotionally, or physically, chances are sex has a part in it.

A Vestal needs to protect herself, psychically and physically! Yes, sex is spiritual, but it is also biological. There are just as many, if not more, physical illnesses as there are psychological and mental illnesses. Because Virgo and Scorpio relate to Vesta, both are spiritual—mind and body. Her main concern is to light a flame, inspire, and give what is needed, but she can lose herself in the process, so she must remain focused and aware at all times.

Vestals are the possessors of mysteries and secrets, and often some dangerous and life-shattering secrets of love and pain. They are meant to harm none; therefore, they must keep secrets and be responsible for themselves, including their sexual health. Vestals must learn about both sides of their nature, which includes reproductive and psychological health.

Vestals can be highly sexual, but they can also be very closed off. They can switch from virgin to whore and back to a virgin by a flicker of fire. They may also have extended periods where they are celibate for years. Celibates are not always sex-free, as we have discussed. Chastity means faithfulness; masturbation happens in celibacy, and chastity in marriage. If we teach abstinence, let masturbation be a part of the curriculum. You do not have to masturbate, but it is perfectly acceptable to touch yourself. Touching is sensual, and self-love matters. Sometimes release is required. Masturbation is also beneficial to relationships.

Sex can be so beautiful, and it can be ugly. Disease is prevalent in much of the world. Even someone who has never had sexual intercourse could still have contracted an STI or illness. Having a disease or infection can have debilitating psychological and physical effects that can worsen health if not handled well. Once you get sick, your health is never the same. The presence of STDs is higher than all other infectious diseases in the world. They are more common than the flu; therefore, feel no shame. However, group therapy and discussions are available for support.

Keeping your immune system healthy is imperative to sustain life. Lessen your exposure to illness and protect yourself. Just as you do not want to cook when you are sick, you do not want to have sex when you are sick. By managing vaginal pH, one is aware of the things that enter into the body. Many things can alter pH, from the food we eat to the clothes we wear. Women are more sensitive than men in contracting an STI and tend to have more complications, and are therefore advised to take more care and concern with their sexual health.

The whole body requires air to breathe and live. Fire needs oxygen to survive as does Vesta. All are divine and aware of their needs, and they are all creators, sustainers, and destroyers. Which to choose in the present comes from the consciousness within. Once made, conscious intent follows.

Romantic feelings can lead many to assume that they will be with "the one" for the rest of their lives. Romance leads to taking more risks than what would be considered healthy, hence a Vestal is encouraged to stay out of romantic involvement. A Vestal has a duty; she helps her home and community through involvement and political influence. She understands that the health of the individual is part of the health of the community. Ideally masturbation is encouraged. Sexual health and safe sex talked about, and sexual transmutation (how to turn sexual desire into spiritual devotion, artistic expression, or viable projects) studied early in life.

The word "venereal" is Latin for sexual love and stems from Venus. Some may say that the 6th, 7th, and 8th houses/temples are the ones which indicate a possible 'venereal' disease: Virgo, Libra, Scorpio, and their corresponding planets; Mercury/Chiron/Vesta, Venus, Mars/Pluto. The 6th temple is below the surface, the 7th temple is relating, the 8th temple is the hidden that may become known through others, death, and sex, for example. Not everyone who has one of these placements has or will get an STD, however.

Viruses and bacteria coexist with the rest of us; there may be more of these cells in our bodies than our own. Vestals must be aware, honest, and compassionate when faced with those that exist, both those living in the body and the disembodied. Others exist within us and outside of us. As the story goes: life is a sexually transmitted disease; keep on living, or get busy dying!

More on Sexual Healing

Often a Vestal's celibacy is involuntary. With discipline, one may come to accept their abstinence. Vesta rules the art of finding a sexual outlet, being sexy to heal sexuality. Finding your sexuality through expressing sex can work sometimes in a nonsexual way: erotic dancing, painting, gardening, ritualized festivities, or whatever turns her on, that is her sacred work.

Masturbation can bring a sense of guilt when in a relationship. Why would anyone want to feel that? Jealousy is a workable problem. Masturbation is something we all do whether or not we are in a partnership. Self-love must be honored in any relationship. To love yourself is to love another.

How one feels about sexuality and reproductive parts says a lot about a person. People may have feelings of fear, guilt, shame, or other negative emotions based on the idea of sex. To heal these sexual dysfunctions, we must use sex. It is vitally important to express ourselves sexually in the way we want to feel sexy. Tantra is a great sexual healing tool and can be done by yourself or with a loving, open partner. An alternative to Tantra may be BDSM, another form of sexual healing. The book *Dark Moon Rising: Pagan BDSM and the Ordeal Path* by Raven Kaldera is a good source that links BDSM with ritual spirituality and sexual healing.

Many people cannot open up (physically, emotionally, or spiritually) to just anyone. It takes time and the ability to trust someone. The body is a temple; it is sacred and does not allow entrance to just anyone. Fear, anxiety, pain, shame, guilt, etc., have debilitating effects on the psyche, emotional, and physical body. Broken trust causes pain in the physical and spiritual body.

A person who knows herself well will notice all of her sensations and will listen to them. If she is attracted to someone, she will want to explore this attraction. That does not mean she wants to go straight to bed with that person. When you let someone into your bed, you are letting them entirely into your sacred space. That includes their physical, emotional, and spiritual selves.

Sexual predators (Priapus) get castrated by society; everyone seems to be sexually wounded by society. We need Vesta to help us heal. She also heals the sexual predator, diseases, and mishaps or misunderstandings. When we study the nature of our sexuality and desire, we can do the work that needs to be done rather than suppressing it into repulsion.

Yoni Tantra

Liberation is achieved through enjoyment. Happiness is gained through enjoyment. Therefore, by every effort, a sadhaka should become an enjoyer. The wise man should always avoid blame, disgust, or shame of the yoni. Unless the yoni is worshipped using the Kulachara method, even one hundred thousand sadhanas are useless.

Hindu culture teaches, through the caste system, that Brahmins hold the highest spiritual authority, but finding a true Brahmin depends on astrology, not caste. Brahmins, in astrology, are usually those with their Moon in a water sign (Cancer, Pisces, Scorpio). Brahmins are priests(esses) and scholars. They are often saintly and not necessarily part of the Brahmin Indian Caste. Water signs are the most fluid and receptive. A water Moon sign is the most psychic of all the Moon signs. In the Kundalini rising astrology charts, all had either a water moon sign or their moon was in a house under the influence of water. The moon was either in Cancer, Scorpio, or Pisces, or the moon is in either the 4th, 8th, or 12th temple.

They say that a Brahmin girl should worship her *yoni tattva* or menstrual cycle. The concept of the sacred *Yoni tattva* is a yoni mantra or a ritual to the sacred feminine aspects in Kaula Tantra. It is a secret sadhana that few know about and is not often translated into Western text. Understandably, it is done alone; however, there is also a partner ritual (the first menstrual cycle after marriage). Many associate it with a ritualized drink mixture of menstrual blood or female ejaculation (Amrita), perhaps semen, and ghee or milk. The ritual may occur during the night of the full moon at a quarter cross point.

Dearest, if by good fortune one is partner to a Brahmin girl, one should worship her yoni tattva. Otherwise, worship other yonis. When we speak of Brahmin, here we speak about those who are Brahmin by birth based on Astrology, and not because one is born in a Brahmin home.

Candali, Lady of Hosts, the foremost one, is the center of the yoni. By worshiping in this way, one becomes my equal, most certainly. What use are meditations, reciting mantras, giving gifts, or kula nectars? O Durga, without yoni worship, all are fruitless.

This ritual drink is considered the drink of the gods, perhaps similar to the intoxicating substance Vedic priests used in their rituals. The Romans called it ambrosia, the Greeks called it nectar, and the Hindus call it Amrita, Amata, or Soma. There are many stories of the gods and devas having to fight to protect the divine drink. This Amata or nectar is said to give strength, power, transcendence, and immortality. There is another story that the Amata was saved from the mortals and replaced with alcohol.

It is better to be virtuous than to perform rites or rituals. Vestals keep some things secret, and the Yoni Tantra is one sacred rite which is not for everyone. The reason is love. No one experiences love in the same way, so how could a yoni mantra be performed the same way and have any power? In general, the rite would include a mantra. 108 is the number of times the mantra (however you decide to create it) continues before allowed entrance into the womb/Universe.

...there are people who regard semen and menstrual fluid with disgust, but they forget that the body by which they hope to attain Liberation is composed of these two forms of matter, that the marrow, bone, and tendons have come from the father and the skin, flesh and blood from the mother. It further says that there is no reason for man's disgust for excreta or urine, for

these are nothing but food or drink which has undergone some change and contains living creatures and the Brahman substance is not absent therefrom ... All things are pure. It is one's mentality which is evil. (The Kaulavali Nirnaya, pp 19-20. Agamanusandhana Samiti, Calcutta.)

Sacred Rites and Relics of Vesta

> *"Work is auspicious, work is beautiful, but it is not the end. This is an alpha but not an omega. One has to go beyond this. But going beyond it is not condemnation. To go beyond this, one has to pass through this. Tantra keeps the healthiest vision towards work." ~Unknown*

It is in the womb where every new being, beginning, idea, and intention happens. It is where those who want full expression in the material world enter. There is work to do, and rebirth is required to complete that work. Vesta provides the space needed for entry into the divine duty.

Vesta protects the sanctity of the womb/house (body), the sacred hearth/creativity (fire), and the family and community (empire). She is untouchable, filled with perpetual passion, and brings energy to her everyday work. The ultimate domestic goddess, she is a temple all on her own.

Vestals were sacred and trusted with all that is sacred. They were present at every festival and rite. The holiest items of Rome, which the fate-of-the-nation depended upon, were guarded by the Vestals. A shrine built in the center of the Atrium called the Penetralia is the innermost sanctuary of Vesta. The high Priest/Pontifex Maximus is the only man permitted to enter this sacred space. Only on day one of the festival Vestalia were women of the public allowed to pass the threshold of Vesta's temple. They would come in their most wretched forms to ask the goddess to grant their desire. (Vestalia is Vesta's holiday from June 7-15th.; a week's worth of festivities.)

Temple relics were kept in sealed earthen jars placed next to other sealed earthen pots which held grain and foodstuffs. One of these relics was the sacred Palladium. Minerva/Athena, friend of Pallas, won a wrestling match in which Pallas died. Minerva felt terrible and made a statue of her friend and competitor. Presented to Jupiter, he threw it to the Earth, where it landed in the hands of a man praying for a sign. Where Pallas landed was the location where the city of Troy was built.

The statue was thought to be made of wood carved as a woman with long draperies hanging to her feet. In her right hand was a spear and in her left was a spindle and distaff; together they showed the unity of male and female energies. It was said that whichever city possessed the Palladium would never be conquered. The Goddess Pallas is a creative warrior who can make pretty or utilitarian things and also join in the battle.

Vestals also had to be cleansed. They may have done so at the end of their shift of guarding and controlling the sacred flame, and perhaps before. They were bread makers, and were required to bake salsa mola, a special cake, to bless the sacrificial animals.

Touch and care from the hands of the Vestals were sacred. The holiest of the holy, Vestals cared for all the relics used in the festival. They prepared their cakes (mola salsa or flour-and-salt) cleanly and simply applying the strictest rules, including water from the sacred spring in its purest form. They picked the first ears of corn and dried them, pulverizing the grain into fine flour using a mortar, or by a donkey turning a grindstone. They prepared the cakes with salt and purified the substance by fire in a kiln oven. Many rites or rituals of ancient times included animal sacrifices, and the Vestals purified the animals. It was their job to dress the animals, gutting and cleaning in preparation for cooking the flesh.

Once a year at the equinox, the Vestals ritually extinguished the sacred fire and cleansed the temple with sacred water from a spring in the depth of the forest. The filth and ash were carried to the Tiber River for disposal. (Anything unclean, including people, would be tossed into the Tiber. The Romans sometimes dropped their criminals into it for the gods to deal out their fate.) On the first day of Vestalia, fresh laurel was gathered from the temple of Mars, and the temple of Vesta was adorned with laurel wreaths and garlands hung everywhere. The donkeys, sacred to Vesta, were given time to rest, decorated with wreaths and flowers, and given cakes and loaves of bread.

The temple of Vesta was covered in food offerings to the Goddess and the fire was ritually relit by the Pontifex Maximus. In the oldest times, he would rub two pieces of wood together until they ignited (hence the importance of keeping the fire lit). (I learned to do this with flint and steel.) Later, glass was used to focus the Sun's rays and spark a flame. It is said that the Pontifex Maximus was the only one who could light the fire of Vesta.

On the last day, Penetralia, the temple was opened to the public and offerings were brought in exchange for the Vestals' blessing(s). Women came to the temple at this time to pray for their hearts' desire, or for happy hearths and homes. Renunciates today are still brought gifts and donations for their prayers and blessings; many monks and nuns live off of the charity from their patrons.

Any reason to celebrate is a reason to live! Vestals celebrate the seasons and astrological events. Many saints' days Vestals commemorate have ancient origins, such as Lupercalia. This festival takes place on the full moon before the 15th of February and is associated with Fauns and Priapus as well as other holidays. "Lupus", or the wolves and wild dogs that preyed on the goats or sheep were sacrificed to at this time. It was also a fertility festival later linked to the Feast of the Purification, and associated with Saint Valentine's day. During this ritual sacrifice, the ritual blood was cleansed with the mother's milk. After the ritual feast, the men cut thongs from the skins of the animals and then ran through the city, striking any woman who neared them in order to make them fertile. It was considered good luck to be spanked with the hide of the sacrificial animal. Since it was the Vestals' duty to purify every ritual, cleaning and dressing the animal was their duty.

Vesta is always present, both steady and grounded as an Earth goddess, and as untouchable and constantly moving as a fire goddess. She stays connected with her feminine aspects through the daily grind of mundane life and the work required to attain her most ambitious spiritual goal.

Vesta is of the earth and is the fire. People are drawn to fire. (It is said that in the case of rape, it is advisable to yell "fire" as more people would come then if one screamed "rape".) If Priapus took her virginity, it would only be fair for her to take something of his, hence the sacred phallus. The divine phallus was one of the celestial relics held in her temple; it was said to reside in a secret place and was a fascinating magical object which possessed fertility powers and would appear in the hearth of the sacred fire. There are many stories about the *fascinus* (divine phallus), including that Vestals gave out small phallic items representing the *fascinus* as tokens or amulets of good luck. Virgins were said to get pregnant by it; it was not unheard of for a Vestal, nun, or other woman to become impregnated by the sacred phallus. There are temple priestesses in other cultures who also worship gods or phalli.

The Vestal initiation included a sacred marriage, the rite of *captio*[13]. In Roman times this may have been like an adoption, leaving one family for another. Many modern nuns and priests consider initiation a marriage to Goddess, God, or Christ.

Their vows included submission to serve the goddess (and the Pontifex), obey her, and protect Rome. A Vestal learned her duties and how she was to worship and initiate. Her life was to be pure and simple. Taking vows is often difficult, however, and they are often tested by Life. Promises are hard to keep. By making vows, the Vestal strengthens her character. Exercising her willpower, she vows to aid in facilitating growth.

> "...*Twenty little girls [chosen by] the Pontifex Maximus... [he] spoke to her [on] the grave duties ... "I take thee, Beloved."... no longer a member of her own family, [she] belonged to the sacred sisterhood of Vesta, over whom the High Priest watched with a father's protecting care."*
>
> Stories in Stone from the Roman Forum, Isabel Lovell

Amata or "Beloved" was the title given to the youngest Vestals; the word has many meanings. For a Vestal, it means both "captured matron" and "invincible maiden". *Vestalis Maxima* was the title of the

---

[13] R. L. Wildfang, *Rome's Vestal Virgins*

eldest high priestess and Mother Superior, the dress of the most braided hair. At one time, the number of braids increased as the Vestal became more experienced. Although six braids were typical for the Vestals, the style changed throughout the years. Today, the Vestal designs herself—she is one with her appearance and powerful for it. She can be seen as vibrant and alive, covered in her holy attire. From bread-making to political/religious involvement, every act of a Vestal is sacred and sanctified.

No statue of Vesta resided inside the temple; within lay only the hearth and the flame. However, a shrine depicting her human-like form stood outside the temple. Donations and offerings of food and wine were left near the shrine as no one was allowed to enter her temple.

The Vestals sprinkled the temple and the city daily with holy spring water. Laurel branches were sacred to the gods and make good kindling or fire-starters. Ancient huts were created or blessed with laurel branches much like a sukkah, the sacred hut which Jews build during Sukkot, Feast of Booths.

The laurel tree is known as the goddess's tree. The God Apollo chased Daphne, who turned into a laurel tree, to escape marriage. The tree was still trembling upon his arrival, to which he said, "Since thou canst not be my wife, thou shalt be my tree!" Apollo, crowned with a laurel wreath, and his bow and lyre made from her wood. The virgin's tree is made sacred by the celestial fire god of the Sun. Vesta is the never-dying flame.

Her animal totem is the ass, and her flower is lavender, which was named for the Latin word for washing—it is the cleansing herb. Salt and finely ground grain are sacred to her. On holy days the Vestals make cakes from their special mola salsa and offered them to Vesta and devotees. Vesta is the Fornax/sacred furnace, the spirit of the baker's oven and the potter's kiln.

Mirrors are also a sacred relic of Vesta, although many nuns today live without mirrors. Vesta is not necessarily vain, although a Vestal may use a mirror to see exactly, who she is. Mirrors reflect the sacred fire and hold space. Vestals may have used mirrors for diverting the evil eye, scrying, or self-exploration.

Vesta or a Vestal stands by her power. Represented in the tarot as Strength (Trump 9 or 11), kindly closing the jaws of the lion, she controls her animal nature for a higher spiritual purpose. She can tame her wild desire or be overwhelmed by it.

Contacting Prana Life Energy

This exercise is an integral part of Vestal training, similar to Reiki or hands-on healing. It is also the technique used for distance healing. It begins with healing the self, and then one may extend it to others.

Stand in "star pose". Spread your feet apart, just wide enough that you still feel supported. Raise your arms and separate them about the equal distance as your legs, but still in a comfortable position. Your palms should face forward with fingers spread wide. Stand on your tiptoes for an extra stretch as you reach for the stars. The five points of the feet, hands, and head form a star. From star pose, return your heels to the ground and ground yourself into the Earth. Lower your arms enough to be parallel to the earth and sky. The left palm faces the sky while the right palm faces the ground, another variation of the star pose.

While in this pose, focus on your breath. With each inhalation, focus on *prana* (life energy) entering the body through your left hand. With each exhalation, focus on prana exiting the body through your right hand. Practice this exercise daily until you learn to feel this energy exchange. You can then begin to store this energy in your solar plexus and access it at Will, and recharge as necessary.

Let your breath follow the flow of the life energy; as you breathe in, the breath of life flows into you. As you breathe out, the energy flows out. Feel it flow in through your left palm and flow out of your right. Fill your solar plexus (area near the navel). The solar plexus is your powerhouse and your energy storage area. Put your hands on your belly and feel it expand with universal life as you breathe in and contract as you breathe out. Just focusing on the breath can energize the mind/body.

Every morning upon awakening, stand in star pose and focus on your breath. Breathe the life force in and breathe it out. When you breathe in, concentrate on light and love entering your body. On the exhalation, send that light and love out into the world. Focus it on what you want to heal, and send the energy there. It takes practice, but once you know how to take in and move *prana*, you can send it out into the world. You can heal yourself and others by projecting this loving energy. It does not work when there are blocks, however. I recently released my love from above/life energy out into the world. It felt so wonderful! However, not long after I sent it, I felt like half of it hit a wall—a dark spot. Half of it was blocked.

You cannot heal those who block healing. Some people are so dark in self-loathing that they close themselves off from receiving healing. They need to come out of their grief, fear, shame, self-doubt, or what-have-you if they are to receive the healing that they desperately need. We can take small steps to help them; however, it can waste energy until they are ready to help themselves. Many people must go through the "dark night of the soul" before they are willing to accept the light. Do not take it personally.

Air Ritual

Breathing expresses the voice of the soul, and fire breathing is a powerful practice. Hatha yoga teaches us to breathe in and to breath out while using the "ha" sound. Practice breathing and notice the fire entering and exiting your body as you inhale and exhale. As you breathe in, imagine that it is your first breath of air after being delivered from the womb or buried in earth. Reach the surface and breathe.

Breathe deep into your abdomen, filling the lowest pockets first, all the way up to the highest in the chest. Release your breath, as if to surrender unto death, as though it was your last exhalation. Breathe deep again, focus more on the intake, and just let the outtake happen.

Breathe for life. After some time of rhythmic breathing, you can hold the inhalation for as long as you can. Release and continue the circular breath in a constant flow. After some time, hold onto the exhalation. As you hold on, feel the fresh oxygen flow through your blood and energize the parts of the body it reaches. Exhale and repeat. It is great to give yourself an hour to practice any ritual or meditation.

Fire Ritual

Dancing or cooking around the fire can be a powerful fire meditation. For the simplest fire meditation, use a red candle. The flame should be lower than the eyes, about chest to head high. You can move closer or further away if need be. An arm's length is good if you can control the height. Make sure that the atmosphere is calm, so the flame is still. Open your eyes and focus enough to be able to picture the flare in the mind's eye. You may close your eyes and repeat a mantra. An example may be:

> *By fire, air, water, ether, and earth, I ignite this flame on heart and hearth. I call forth the vitality, the force of the sacred flame, my creative source. I awaken my deepest passions, Through my inner hearth of Earth. I find my true path and steady my course.*

While focusing on the flame, notice its shape and colors. Concentrate on the brightest part of the flame. Close your eyes and hold the image in your mind for as long as you can without causing stress or tension. If it dissipates, open your eyes and repeat. Concentration and focus will increase gradually. This meditation is of short duration and should only last up to about 4 minutes. Other fire meditations can last longer if you will. Fire rituals are fast, high-energy workouts, so make sure that you take rest before exhaustion sets in.

Trancedance is my favorite fire meditation. Like a whirling dervish, I can spin around in circles without losing my balance. I follow the beat to my favorite music and get into the flow. Once connected with the vibration, one rides the waves while the internal fire increases. There is nothing but the music, you, and source. Dance until you drop or break through!

Water Ritual

A ritual bath or cleansing with water is a must for a Vestal. As an element of great symbolism and potent purging, free-flowing water is the purifying ritualization of rinsing away energetic pollutants.

Bathe in a hot bath until relaxed, or the water begins to feel tepid. Be sure to submerge fully underwater at least once. Like a baptism, let yourself go, and what is not yours washes away. Release all, even if you have to think about it first. The hot water is for burning and sweating out toxins. It is the time to let the mind wander or focus on all the things that need to be released. Then access that which belongs to you—hopefully, by this point, what is not yours has melted away. Cry, let go, have a pity party for yourself, and accept yourself as you are. Wash away the dirt, rinse clean, and bless yourself by anointing yourself with oils, lotion, or whatever you do when you finish bathing.

A swim in the river or a dip in the spring connects us with nature. It is your ritual; do it how you see fit. Pray to God or Goddess, thank him/her, make a magic spell, cut cords, do what you will. Be present with yourself and do what feels right for you.

Earth Ritual

Earth ritual for Vestals is housekeeping and gathering of food. At the end of every year, the ancient Vestals would ritually extinguish the sacred fire and clean the hearth and temple. Cleaning out the clutter, dusting, mopping the floor; these are all Earth rituals. Working in the garden, exposure to Nature, and talking to trees and plants are also Earth rituals. Grounding exercises are great! Circles of salt, salt lamps, and other minerals are purifying and related to the Earth. Here is one that incorporates the elements.

If your environment is friendly, step outside and stand with your feet against Gaia. Feel through your feet and toes. Is the ground cool, soft, or squishy? How does it make you feel? Stand in a comfortable, stable position, legs apart. Raise your arms parallel to the ground, with your left palm facing up, right palm facing down. You can close your eyes or leave them open. Be aware of your surroundings. Breathe. Take deep, cyclical breaths. With each inhale, you are bringing energy and awareness into your being. With each exhale, you are grounding your energy into Her through your feet. Do this for 30 breaths and then hold. As you pause your inhalation, be aware of yourself and your relationship to Gaia. Release and repeat for as long as you need. I usually reserve an hour for meditation, but this exercise can be done in minutes and worked into longer sessions over time.

As a Vestal, business owner, wife, and mother, I know how difficult it can be to carve out some time to be alone, much less time to meditate. It is part of Vesta to take care of ourselves. Burnout serves no one. Vestals must be sound in mind and body. When unbalanced, sore, stressed, or overwhelmed, we must escape to our sanctuary. Close yourself off in your bedroom and tell everyone to leave you alone, if need be. Allow yourself time to recharge. Heaven can wait. You will thank yourself later.

4/29/2021: I stumbled upon this yoga during the pandemic. We had all gotten sick, and I had vomited. Days later, my mind was full of racing thoughts; I had the worst headache. It felt like a block, pushing through my crown. I stopped doing the nightly rituals and forced myself to go to bed. The house was loud, but I did not care if I drifted in and out of sleep. I let it flow. After about an hour or two, the headache was gone, I was relaxed, and my mind was still.

I have already mentioned the practice of Hatha Yoga and Pranayama (conscious breathwork to enhance life energy). The third practice to mention is Yoga Nidra. Yoga Nidra is the art of rest. As I have said, it is advisable to all, especially Vestals, to give time to rest.

Incense

Incense is often a part of rites and rituals. Frankincense and Myrrh, used by the ancients, are still used today in places like the Catholic church. "Darshan" is my incense of choice. Darshan is said to deepen devotion and open doorways to the divine in purity and love. I use it because it smells nice (no one has complained otherwise), and it motivates me to move, exercise my mind/body, and cleanse my house.

Stones

Pyroxene is Vesta's mineral. Rich in iron and magnesium, it is a mafic, igneous rock, a form of volcanic glass. Pyroxene is heat-resistant and used in many things today, such as ceramics, medication, and lithium batteries used in cell phones and electric cars. Pyroxene in Greek means "stranger in a false illusion" or "fire and stranger". There are many forms of Pyroxene. It is also known as actinolite, augite pyroxene, chlorite, epidote, spodumene, etc.

Spodumene means "burnt to ash" and is specifically lithium-rich Pyroxene. It is one of many minerals used in ceramics and glaze, bringing out the copper tones of the minerals in the glaze mix. Spodumene reduces the thermal expansion of the mix and reduces the contraction (shrinkage) of the clay. Spodumene for lithium batteries is in high demand during our technical times. The pink form is *kunzite*, a protector of the heart. The green form is *hiddenite*, which represents creation and living in the present. The yellow form is *triphan*, which cleanses and gets rid of energies that compromise the body.

Spodumene is one of my favorite stones for representing Vesta. It helps to detach from dependencies and inspires emotional healing. It is a modern Vestal's protector from intrusive forces, gives her confidence, and keeps her present. It allows free space for creative and emotional support. It is a shield against confrontation, aggression, and anxiety.

Spodumene is used for restructuring the RNA and DNA, healing on a cellular level. It has been used to treat STIs and can align all major Chakras quickly. It offers comfort and solitude and brings newfound lust for life. Spodumene helps relieve emotional blocks that hold you back from experiencing the positive emotions of life.

Obsidian is another firestone which is also associated with Vesta. Lava from deep inside the Earth bursts through and flows on earthen surfaces. When this lava cools rapidly, it transmutes into obsidian. Because of quick cooling, the crystals have no time to form, and the rock becomes like black glass; hence the name, volcanic glass.

Other stones include meteorites—howardites, eucrites, and diogenites. Some may even have come from the asteroid Vesta, possibly from a meteor impact to her basin Rheasilvia.

Food Preservation

Vestals are known for their cooking. Vesta's hidden powers of preservations are often disregarded; she represents our basic survival needs which so many take for granted. The ancient Vestals gathered nuts, seeds, and grain, pulverizing their harvest into fine powder. The flour or cornmeal could be kept and used at a later time. They purified and refined salt, which they used to make brine. Combining the salt and flour together they created polenta, unleavened bread, matzoh, cakes or mola salsa. Today we may add butter or oil for flavor.

Salt comes from sea or mineral water, and it takes a lot of water to make a little salt. The water is collected and left to settle, allowing sediment to fall, and then is strained through a sieve and into a pot. Over low heat, the saltwater simmers. Overheating can cause the salt to burn or stick, so the process requires many hours or days attending the fire. When most of the water has evaporated, the pot is removed from the heat. The ancient Vestals were said to have put the salt slurry into sealed clay vessels, and then into the fire to finish the refining/evaporating process. Distillation is a purifying way commonly used for many things, including salt, water, oils, and alcohol. A lid catches the condensation, and the water is also purified.[14] Condensation

---

[14] History of Distillation - ScienceDirect
https://www.sciencedirect.com/science/article/pii/B9780123865472000016

is potable water when the water is from a pure source. Ancient Vestals had underground food storage areas where they kept the preserved food.

To make brine for preservation, mix one part refined salt to 16 parts purified water (one cup salt to one gallon of water). Some herbs and spices may be added to the brine. Cover the meat or vegetable with the brine and refrigerate. Can it or put it into sealed pots. For fermentation, cover it but leave it unsealed. Let it set unattended until bubbles rise to the surface (in about three days), then refrigeration or sealing will be needed.

The history of unleavened bread has to do with sacrifice. When the Hebrews left Egypt, they did not have time to allow the yeast to rise. Yeast became linked with sin, and therefore to have bread without yeast was considered a sacrifice. Matzoh, as unleavened bread, is still used today to commemorate the exodus from Egypt. However, many ancient peoples, including the ancient Vestals, were known for their unleavened bread, mola salsa, ground grain and salt.

Eating is more than a daily ritual; many people have a set time for meals. There is a time in the morning when we break our fast. Midway through the day, we have lunch to fuel us until the evening and the last meal of the day. These are sometimes the only moments where people come together as a group, pray, and/or give thanks to god/goddess. The everyday things count; gatherings around the hearth, prepping for dinner, and enjoying the meal.

Vesta can be honored before and after a meal. Meals, as well as other creations, are made with love, care, and devotion. If one is ill, they should not make the meal but should be cared for by another until they are well enough to return to their station. Vestals are there to help. It is how a Vestal fulfills her role in her community. She heals the ill in subtle and mysterious ways.

Modern Vestal Women and Sexuality

Vestals must guard themselves against attachment, as their lives are meant to be lived simple and free. Because they may inadvertently go around sparking passion in people, they may have to put across energy saying that they are unavailable. Passion is addicting, and women may want to attach themselves to the person who awakens these passions inside. However, it is not the person but the passion that moves us, and that needs to be understood. Once we start living for another, our flame subsides. Attachment is like ash. Over time when the ash builds, the fire weakens. You will need to periodically clean out the ash to have a fire that can breathe.

In our modern and sex-troubled culture, it's not uncommon that when a man does something nice for a woman, there is a kind of stigma around it. Either the man expects something in return, or the woman feels obligated to give something in return. However, Vesta is about sex only when the focus is on sex, and not on cultural assumptions.

Some Vestal women who have heterosexual intercourse and have a man's ejaculation released into them may bear the inconvenience of sensing the gunk build-up which the man has been carrying around. Highly sensitive Water-sign Vestals may experience it more readily than others. Early sex-negative programming aside, this may be a partial cause of why some women feel "yucky" after sexual intercourse when they felt fine just before the act. This experience may be the cause of why many Vestal women must retreat after this kind of sex. They must learn to distinguish energetically between what is theirs and what is someone else's, and not to be held onto. A good soak in the healing waters can wash away the energy of the other person and bring her healing and cleansing.

Vesta teaches us to use both our feminine and masculine power. She is confident in her sexuality and has enough self-respect to assert her Will, and so should a modern Vestal. The deal is between the Vestal and the Goddess; no other. The Vestal's first loyalty is to Vesta.

She is all that is physical, mental, and spiritual. She creates, destroys, and sustains. Kings come and go, but a Vestal remains the same. She is steadfast and unwavering.

In Kabbalah, they say that desire does not come from us. Desires exist only to receive the gift or the pleasure the Creator wants to bestow on us. Modern Vestal women may choose to give a devotee their desire, or to give pleasure through the fulfillment of desire, but what the Vestal provides is not always what the devotee expects. A trained Vestal woman, refined in her mind, body, and emotions, closes the mouth of the ravenous lion. She has control of the animal instinct and she knows how to wield its power, transcending the lower energies to a higher plane. By making Earthly desires pure, she constructs them into higher energy channels that benefit all involved. Like Jacob's ladder, Malkuth transcends to Keter, and the cycle begins again on a higher vibration, level, or rung of the ladder.

Typically, the Vestal woman will encounter many with only the desire for immediate sense gratification, and she may choose to help free them from their limiting existence. Using her feminine powers, subtly assisting them in realizing their errors, the Vestal encourages them to seek their higher selves. She is careful not to engage in the bestial sense but to use those desires in a purely constructive way—that is, turning a temporary desire for immediate gratification into a lasting, fulfilling one.

Vestals are very aware of subtle psychic energies that go unnoticed by non-initiates. They may talk to trees or animals, experience clairaudience, or sense telepathy, because they are receptive and aware. Other living things have a profound effect on a Vestal, and she must retreat and cleanse to recharge herself and dissipate energies that have attached themselves to her.

A Vestal should be reliable and resourceful. She is committed to her duty and will see it through to the end; focused dedication will take her far. Attending the fire can help when she loses focus, gets confused, or feels like giving up. Finding her center is required, and fire meditation is the most helpful, including dancing around a fire.

However, in the end a Vestal should use all five elements, as Vesta is the beginning and end of all rites and rituals. Earth, air, water, fire, ether (space) can all be utilized by a Vestal.

The Vestal Rite of Power

If a modern Vestal chooses to give her devotee their desire, she must remember that Vestals can only offer so much of themselves due to their unique vows. They must provide the devotee as much of their desire as is possible without compromising their sacred selves. This skill comes with much refinement and practice. The Vestal must know how to be dominant in all situations to keep herself sacred and free of attachments. She is always to refrain from giving all of herself. When the devotee seeks what she cannot offer, she must find a way without compromising herself, or refuse. Now is where her creativity and determination come through. Sometimes she will need the help of other Vestals, or maybe even introduce the devotee to their future spouse.

The goal here for the Vestal is objectivity, and to become an embodiment of this objectivity. How does she view the world? She must go deep into her experiences and find the truth of the matter. Once free from subjectivity through self-actualization, she can be truly independent. However, when she lets too many into her fire, they can smother it. Free your mind and allow your passion to flow through you and out of you, creating or destroying your own life. Fire breathing and making contact with prana/life energy are tools to utilize for this purpose.

Vesta easily opens and closes the mouth of an angry, hungry, or passionate lion. She is the spiritual, grounding force and emanates strength controlling the violent forces of nature. She lives a pure, innocent life and has faith in herself. Her love is spiritualized and she knows and understands her power. She holds the animal's power that flows through her.

Compassion

A Vestal's role, however, is not about dominance of power. It is about compassion. Compassion means "to suffer with". As a bodhisattva, Vestals are compassionate. In Buddhism, a bodhisattva has reached enlightenment but decided to reincarnate again to help humanity. Vestals often volunteer to participate freely in the joys and sufferings of others. Suffering is a part of life. As part of the duality of the world, joy and pain are facts. By accepting suffering as it is, one can transmute it into creative power. Vestals learn this process, and they can teach others.

Some modern-day Catholic and Buddhist nuns believe that "passion" means to suffer, and some nuns believe that the point of their suffering is to help lost souls, to be kind and compassionate to wrongdoers so much so that they are willing to suffer themselves to lift evildoers—even those in the afterlife. They forgive the sins of the flesh. Vestals see good in everyone.

If one achieves emptiness, one no longer suffers, but one no longer feels joy or anything else. It is not a state of mind that all can live in. If we are to live on this plane of existence, we must accept pain, as well as happiness, but we can enter emptiness when we choose. Most of us want to experience the highs and lows of the world; that is why we are here. Sorrow does not have to keep us down. Vestals use distress as part of alchemical transmutation.

The inverted triangle is one of her symbols. Will, knowledge, and activity represent the three points or angles, just as Vesta exercises her Will, gains knowledge, and acts on her highest devotion. The six-pointed star represents the union of masculine and feminine; it is the union of the upward and downward facing triangles.

Tantra

Body tingling, sensual vibrating, being with Earth, the living, breathing, heart-pumping, joy of pleasure in the simplest of things; Tantra!

Tantra has passed through dirty hands since around 1500-1700 BCE. It has taken on many shapes and forms, but Tantra is still highly shrouded in secrecy. Ancient people were more grounded with Gaia than many are today. The Dravidians of southern ancient India (not necessarily linked to today's Dravidians) were tree worshipers.[15] It is not too far-fetched to say that they communicated with trees. The Dravidians' civilization is where most ancient Hinduism is derived from. In the West, Tantra is thought of as a sex cult or religion, but Tantra is not just about sex or religion; Tantra is about all systems of life. Sex is only one part. Tantra is about the joyful experience of life, the celebration and ritualization of all things physical, including people, joys, sorrows, plants, animals, minerals, and their roles and sacred work.

What I have come to understand is that Tantra is "left" or "right". There is no left-handed path or right-handed path, only *the* path. Tantra is a healing and growth process, the experience of loving what is! There is no distinction between good and evil; the wheel is constantly spinning. Tantra is our relationship to the living world.

In this way, Vestals can be like Tantrikas in the Hindu tradition, because a Vestal interacts with others on *her* terms. There are many types of Vestals throughout different religious communities; Catholic nuns, monks, and priests are a form of the Vestal; so sometimes are the priests and priestesses of Pagan religions. A monk, Kabbalist, Thelemite, whirling dervish, heyoka, geisha, sex worker, or Jehovah's Witness may all be types of Vestals found throughout the world.

As I said in the beginning, my guru is very Vestal. Gurus are often gatekeepers or thresholders. They lead the way, but it is your journey.

I wrote about my first experience with Tantra from the guidance of my guru, with just myself and a mirror.

---

[15] https://earlyworldhistory.blogspot.com/2012/03/dravidians.ht ml
https://global.oup.com/us/companion.websites/9780195397703/student/materials/chapter26/

2/17-18/2016. I let it build more quickly. to the point where I held it, and then I changed. The more I held on, the more I changed. Looking at myself, I saw power, immense power. I looked fierce, angry, passionate; it was like a lion inside me was coming out. I felt on fire. I knew this power existed deep inside of me, but I have never seen it before. To sum it up short, I saw Red.! I felt incredibly forceful and horny all day. I did it two more times. I did not say anything to myself; I just observed. The second time I noticed an aura of red hearts ascending from my body after climax. The third time I do not remember. I suppose I just wanted to get off again. Dogma kept creeping up a little, me thinking what I was doing was devilish. I asked for guidance and received assurance that I was growing, and acknowledged that this is an important step. I had a feeling of being blessed.

Healing

You cannot truly feel pleasure without first healing yourself. A Tantric ritual, such as conscious masturbation, can bring up past trauma. Let it come up and move through it; only then can you move past it. Healing takes place, and then the pleasure comes. It is only when we can truly let go of the pain that we can experience bliss. Find what needs healing, and then devote yourself to that healing. When you create, you create with who you are in the moment.

I experienced emptiness. There was no pain, but there was no pleasure. Everything was still; nothing existed. It was peaceful and empty. I appreciated this state for some moments, but my energy is in existence. I must create. I live not to be still, but to be joyful and experience life to the fullest until I am ready again to be still once more. I felt the creative calling of Shakti and the almost sad emptiness of Shiva.

Pleasure feels good and makes us want to live and enjoy life. Pain is protection. Pain tells the person something is wrong and needs correction. When you allow things to unfold and happen, flow is easy and uninhibited; flow leads to liberation. Free your blocks, and Shakti's energy will flow free throughout your life!

Love is used to overcome your opposition. Allowing your magnetism to lead your Will creates your world. A modern Vestal must be free to follow pulls of energy and allow transmutation to occur. She uses her creative powers to transcend man and woman from physical limitations to the higher realms of the spiritual work. She must learn to control her thoughts, as they have power. She can pick up on the thoughts and feelings of others because she is feminine and receptive, and she may also penetrate the minds through her actions or masculine self.

The modern Vestal may be a sacred prostitute, giving herself to others in a loving way, with soulful love, devotion, and a true understanding of freedom. She might be a "virgin", remaining pure by controlling her sexuality. She might put her focus into the divine, art, self-love, her work, etc. Vesta offers her sanctuary to those needing refuge and spiritualizes those that seek her. They may offer wise counsel to those who need it. Most often, a Vestal is sought out consciously or unconsciously by a willing initiate. A Vestal can choose to offer his/her services to those she sees in need or someone worthy of initiation.

An important lesson for a Vestal Virgin is to develop boundaries early on. Vestals are taught to know themselves and what they want and do not want. They will not tolerate violations. Boundaries are too often pushed where Vesta is concerned. It is humorous that Priapus rules boundary lines; this may be why some Vestals need a protector, or a protective group. (The Pontifex Maximus may have acted as such, as well as the temple itself.) To invoke Priapus, one simply needs to erect a giant phallus to protect said boundaries. Sometimes the Vestal has to be a "dick" to guard her sacred space!

However, modern Vestals are not always meant for monogamous relationships. Certainly many can and do enter into relationships, and Vestals can be highly devoted to someone and to sustaining the love between them. But Vesta is not relationship bound; a Vestal virgin must stand in solidarity. She is a pillar of the community. Some ancient Vestals may have chosen to be married after their 30-year service, but generally they did not. Today, it is a challenge to remain independent when having to share in a relationship.

A Vestalis Maxima does give, but only gives what she wants to. She knows not to give herself away; there must be a balance. Universal laws state that you cannot receive without giving. You can receive without giving; however, you will have to pay for it eventually, even if it is just through negative emotions such as resentment. The child that receives everything without having to work becomes resentful to the parents, the ones who gave to them. It is about a balanced exchange of energy. It may be a theme for some Vestals to need to learn.

A Vestal knows that relationships do not last forever. People change, people move, people pass over. To fall in love is only passing, although of course people do find lasting love, but to attach oneself to another is to allow self-destruction. A Vestal must be free, as she enables others to be free.

Vesta extirpates fear. She gives us the confidence needed to be our best selves. Vesta is like Shakti in that she has the power to burn through Chakra blocks and unite the flow of energy throughout the body, which is the beginning of sacred healing. One must always begin with the Root Chakra, the base where kundalini energy resides, when working with the chakras. Through Tantra experiments, we open the doors to ourselves. We become familiar with our erotic nature. The deeper we go into this, the more we can come into our divine selves. There is nothing dirty or wrong with your mind/body. We have desires because they need expression and experience to grow spiritually.

Tantra experiments are great to do with yourself before opening up to a partner. Exploring your body, what turns you on, and what makes you feel good is essential before exploring these things with others. When one knows how to please the self, then one knows what to accept from others. Knowing what you do not like is also important.

If all of your chakras are open and flowing freely, connecting with others becomes natural. You are grounded, wide-open, confident, loving, intuitive, and exhibit a connection to the divine. You know yourself so well that you can control the flow of relations, situations, conversations, and experiences.

Vestals must have an abundance of self-control, because a Vestal's environment affects her psyche. Your body is the channel. Mudras and hand gestures can slow or quicken the pace you chose to move in. Regulating your breath or changing its rhythm has profound effects on others. You can tune yourself into their breath to understand their current energy or bring them into yours. Knowing your feelings and being able to express them with others is the ability of honest communication.

Orgasms can release a lot of baggage (emotional, mental, and physical). It is another area where a Vestal must be aware; if or when she takes this energy as the receiver, she must know how to transmute it. Sometimes what is released is disparaging and can make the Vestal feel bad; this may be why some people may feel negative emotions after having sex or doing healing work. They must recognize that this is not their energy and transmute it into empowerment or a spiritual lesson.

Vestals may need to learn about psychology and manipulation, if only to repel it. Black magic, such as Vidveshana, is another aspect of which a Vestal should be leery, but a Vestal has the power to send it back to the receiver or transmute it and end the spell.

Desires are selfish. Vestals understand this, and they allow others to be selfish. Desire is perfectly natural. You receive cravings so that you can grow to your full potential. There is a reason we crave what we crave, and it would be self-defeating to deny our focus. A Vestal is a priestess of safe, desire fulfillment. People come to the priestess because they want something or need healing. They make an offering, and she provides service. Her interest is in the substance of the divine, home/body, and the divine work of the individual path. When things get too hot, she is the tree that provides shade. Not unlike Lilith, she retreats to the forest.

Virginity and Rape

The story of the Virgin Mary is big-time Vesta! We all know that one cannot biologically impregnate without the other, or in her case, without the "sacred phallus". Some scholars give weight to Mary possibly being raped by a Roman soldier, although most know the story of Mary as being impregnated by God himself. That tends to fit many stories, including the one of Isis and Horus. The donkey was sacred to Mary as it carried her on a journey through her pregnancy.

There has to be a better reason for Priapus' hate of the ass. If my theory is correct, he lost his manhood because of the donkey. He could hardly hate Hestia because she broke his curse and cured him of miserable suffering. Priapus suffered from "priapism", which is a serious condition where the erect penis does not return to its flaccid state and is perpetually hard. It can be extremely painful, and in ancient times the only way to end his suffering was through amputation. Luckily, modern procedures can drain the blood that engorges the penis, and other methods can discern the underlying medical problem and treat it. In Priapus's case, Hera also cursed him with impotence, erectile dysfunction, or the inability to maintain an erection when the opportunity for intercourse arose. He walked around with a hard-on until he sought some relief, but then was denied orgasm.

In my belief, it is most likely that Priapus raped her or tried to rape her, and Vesta, in her Will to not have sex, removed his penis as a service, kindness, or sexual healing. No means no! It does not just pertain to sex. A pushy salesman does not take "no" for an answer. Vesta does not give all of herself into the desires of others. She knows herself, and she knows what she wants. Vesta is kind until someone tries to push their Will against hers. She cuts them off!

In the transit chart of Lorena Bobbitt for July 23, 1993, her natal Priapus asteroid is at 0 degrees Aries. On that night, the famous removal of the penis of her husband John Bobbitt, transiting Nessus was near conjunction to her natal Vesta. She has said that he was a selfish lover, and he had tried to rape her. Nessus is often presented as a planet of abuse and/or ending abuse.

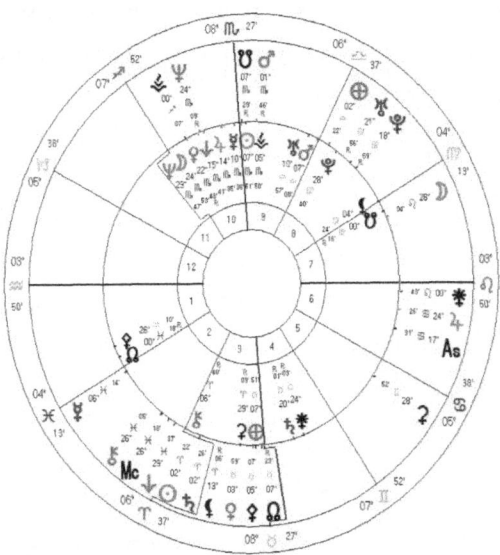

Lorena's natal Vesta is conjunct her natal Sun in a Scorpio stellium. Her sex is sacred to her to the point where she does not share easily. Her Lunar Perigee (a.k.a. Priapus) is at 4 degrees Pisces. These make another aspect to her Sun/Vesta, Chiron, and her nodes. It suggests a destiny and some sexual or genital wounding/healing.

In the transit chart of John Bobbitt for the evening of the incident, transiting Nessus is conjunct his natal Mars in Scorpio (sexual aggression or accidental death). His natal Priapus is conjunct transiting Jupiter, and transiting Priapus, in the sign of the Virgin, is conjunct his natal Pluto and Uranus (a shocking death to manhood). His Lunar Perigee (a.k.a. Priapus) is conjunct the transit chart's Ascendant. Transiting Vesta was conjunct transiting Pallas in Pisces (suggesting gender-role transition). Transiting Vesta is square to the transiting nodes (a period of isolation, hard work, and the need to honor the sacred feminine).

In synastry, Lorena's Neptune is conjunct John's Vesta; perhaps she is romanced by his truth, beliefs, or spirituality. His Mars is conjunct her Vesta; he desired her pure nature. Her moon is conjunct his Neptune—this would suggest a dreamy quality to their relationship—

and his Priapus is conjunct her Mars. The house positions are undetermined. Check out the transit chart by itself! Uranus and Neptune are conjunct at 19 degrees, retrograde in Capricorn, and aspect with Venus square Mars!

In the composite chart for the couple, Vesta is in Scorpio, 7th temple. Pallas, Chiron, and the North Node in the 12th temple are conjunct the Aries point opposite Uranus, the South Node, and the moon in the 6th temple. Their sacred work was their relationship. It is as if their destiny was to come together and work on karmic healing. The story of the Bobbitts is similar to Vesta and Priapus.

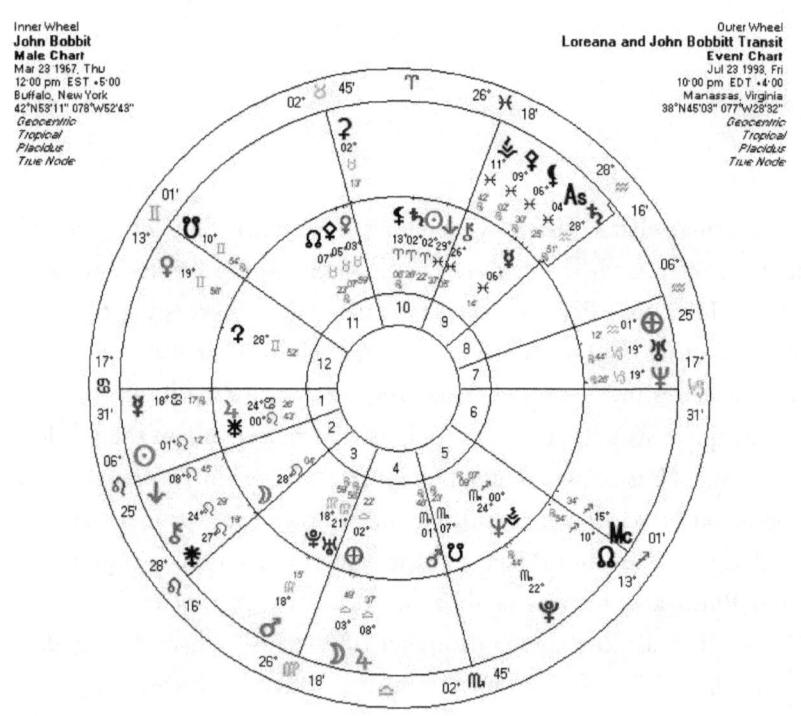

Vesta and Uranus

In mythology both Uranus and Vesta were, at one point, hermits, loners, or removed from their family. Vesta pulls herself out of groupthink, whereas Uranus tends to get ousted by the group. Vesta was almost so voluntarily solitary as to transcend into a tree or eternal flame. Uranus was forced into exile by his family; he buried his children.

Uranus (Sky Father and God of Light) is the mind, the thought, in his head and cut off from the body of Gaia (Earth Mother). Made from Gaia herself, Uranus is her equal and consort. Keeping her impregnated, he would return his children to the earth/womb/fire as soon as they were born.

Uranus fathered Saturn (Cronos), who then castrated Uranus to stop the immoral treatment of Gaia and her beloved children. Although cut off and removed from Gaia, his penis continued to create other powerful gods and goddesses, including Aphrodite, mother of Priapus.

To Vesta, Uranus is the wise, silly, or scary old grandfather. Grandparents and grandchildren have a close connection, often due to the commonality of the generational planets (Uranus, Neptune, Pluto, and Chiron). Biologically, one is their grandparent's child. A woman is born with the eggs created in her mother's womb; the grandchild, conceived through those eggs. Like the buds of a tree are present before the spring of the new year, last year's seedlings become this year's fruit.

Uranus is attracted to those repelled by him, and what Uranus is repelled by is attracted to him. Uranus breaks the Law of Attraction. Like a magnet, Uranus is attracted to its opposite. Though the Law of Attraction is still working, if Uranus follows what feels similar, it is often repelled. Known as Coulomb's Law: "Like charges repel and unlike charges attract." Therefore when Uranus is in opposition to Vesta, it creates friction or a spark that leads to this realization. They are repelled out or pulled in like two reverse magnets.

Vesta is focused intensity; Uranus is unfocused intensity. Aspects between the two in transit make for an introverted or energetically meditative time. It is so intense that the focus is on the inner self, and interactions with the outside world thwarted. Periods of wanting to be touched and wanting to be left alone are typical. Vesta/Uranus types are truly intimate, but they may guard their sacred fire in defense of their mate until they have absolute trust and devotion, which takes time. Too much pressure or invasion into her divine temple(mind/body) feels like rape. Uranus, much of the time, rushes ahead with ideas others do not fully understand. When paired together, the energy is focused, sometimes forced, right now! It is happening! When Vesta surrenders, the magic is activated. Vesta is the center pole where electricity is grounded, and sparks appear. Vesta is the guiding light; Prometheus (a Uranian figure) stole the fire.

Vesta, especially where Aquarius is concerned, is about energy conservation. Vesta represents Fire from the Earth. Uranus rules Aquarius, in the Air element—not in the air that we breathe, but in the endless space of the cosmos. Uranus is the brilliant night that surrounds Gaia in an engulfing blanket of stars and universal knowledge, connecting us to the light and the universal mind.

We are currently in a transitional energy shift. Our focus may be on the element of Air for energy, transportation, and travel. The future of energy is changing, and Uranus is needed to drive that change.

Uranus is self-focused, and eccentric energy often repels. Frequently, Uranus may think too much of their ideals and not enough of others before acting on impulse. The Uranian can have an expressive personality, but the Vestal holds space for him. Sex is a human expression which should not remain demonized or kept hidden. Anyone with a strong Vesta or Uranus presence will have very unusual qualities and desires.

Thank the Uranian Prometheus for the fire! He brings us the ignition. Vesta creates from the spark and fuels the fire. We all have this power and the free will to direct or control it.

Kundalini Rising

As we breathe, the cycle flows; as we hold on, it dies; inhale again, and we are reborn. Breathe deep, and the world around us enters our senses. As we hold it in, our mind expands; inhale again, and become internalized. We feel the world as if it is part of us. Eyes open to vibration, color, and inner consciousness. Living things speak in a language only we can understand.

Vestals are craving and searching for what is unknown to them. If they are unfocused, they tend to be undisciplined in their sacred service. An outside force may often be required for awakening, and spiritually, that can be kundalini rising, which is an objective of some Tantra practices. One who does not know this secret tries to find it in others, possibly indulging in promiscuity, because an undereducated Vestal often seeks Uranus in another. The power to stir this energy is in ourselves, and all Vestals must learn this sooner or later.

Kundalini rising experiences have been documented all over the world. From Christianty to Hindus, kundalini risings occur among many demographics including spiritual and non-spiritual practices. Kundalini rising can be maddening, frightful, exhilarating, psychotic, painful, and/or blissful. It is not unlike ecstasy, but its darker emanations emerge when one does not release control. When allowed, a kundalini rise is and can be a beautiful experience.

Vesta is present in kundalini rise, healing past sexual hurts, emotional blocks, and psychological wounding. By healing these blocks, kundalini can move through the body freely and open us to a new world of identity and realization. Shakti may make us aware of where we concentrate our power.

Kundalini-rise is the exaltation of the ego. After such a spiritual experience one cannot help but feel, at least a little bit, superior. It can also be psychotic as perception is changing. It is conscious-raising amazement, and difficult to come back down from. If it was not for the mundane life, the daily grind to pay bills and take care of business, or the intense changes in perception, I doubt many people would. It is important to keep a spiritual practice through all of this to ground you.

Chakra-focusing exercises are the keys to kundalini rising. Through Tantric meditations like self-loving, chakra balancing, and/or focused intent, transcendence occurs through kundalini rising. The ego, developed fully and consciously, can transmute into devotional service. Vestals learn that, although the flame moves through them, they are not the source. The goddess, Vesta/Shakti, is that source. Before the girls can tend to the sacred flame, they must learn how to ignite or find the inferno. In astrology, it is Uranus that holds the key to spark the eternal flare. Uranus has his placement in every chart, and in my study of kundalini rising transits, it is a prominent natal Vesta in opposition to transiting Uranus that activates it. Things may become subtly interesting when Uranus and Vesta come in aspect to one another on other occasions.

People who have experienced kundalini rise can feel each other whether near or far, if already tuned into the others' energy. The energy between two "risen" people is astonishing. The kundalini energy is thus activated times two! If all the awakened people were to come together on one goal, it would be powerfully accomplished, as the experienced could direct their will and this powerful, energetic force.

The Kundalini Rising Experience

"The eye does not see what the mind does not know."

An astrological birth chart is a tool for understanding when events will occur. Studying the birth charts of people who have experienced a kundalini rise has shown me that Vesta is typically in a stellium. They may have other prominent goddess asteroids or points, including Lilith. At the time of their kundalini rise, natal Vesta is nearly always in opposition to transiting Uranus. Vesta is the energy and creative power; Uranus is the spark. Vesta is the fire inside, the passion for the spirit. She is the yearning that burns. Fire purifies, and it destroys. She is the heat and the vibration. Vesta is Shakti. When activated by Uranus, she pushes through the chakras one by one burning any blockages and illuminates the senses. Rising like an orgasm connecting with the conscious energy, shaking and vibrating, she dances.

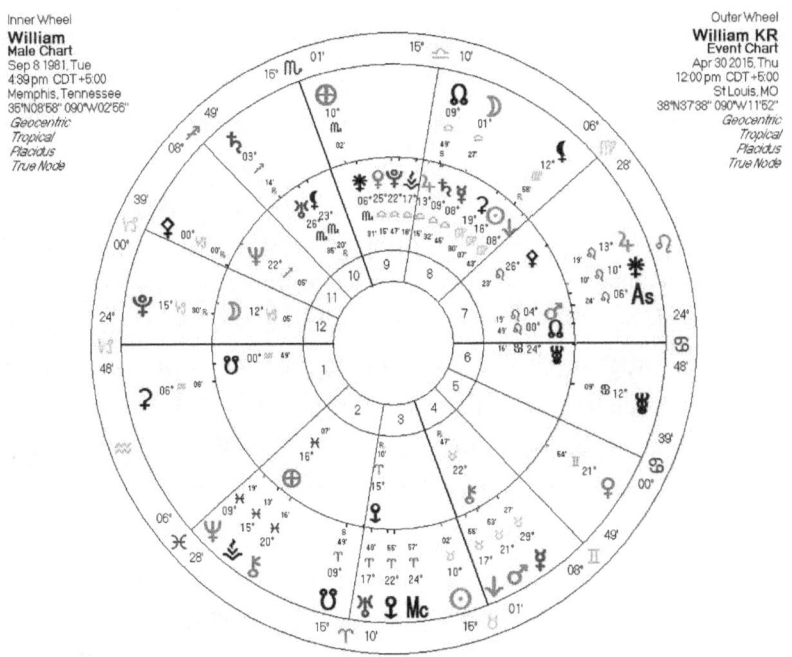

Confusion and anxiousness are part of the kundalini experience. Presented is the kundalini transit chart for William. This person had been experiencing anxiety for three or four weeks before the Kundalini rise (KR). In the chart, we have transiting Uranus conjunct natal Eris/progressed Moon and transiting South Node. Transiting Neptune was square transiting Sun. William is a practitioner of the occult, with natal Sun, Ceres, Mercury, and Saturn in the 8th temple. He was working through some things using study and introspection before experiencing KR. He told me he had an extreme psychedelic mushroom trip a few months prior. Transiting Uranus was opposite natal Vesta at the time of William's KR. He may have experienced this energy more than once due to Uranus' retrograde during that time.

William's Story

William was at work as a bus surveyor, counting and documenting people as they got on and off a bus. Suddenly reality distorted, and William felt as though the bus was driving in and out of hell. Jagged and torn street signs lined the path. A church bus kept driving by ... glitch, glitch, glitch. One of the workers, taking painkillers, offered some to William. To William in the moment, the pills were representations of the presence of the devil; drugs were bad. The bus entered a rough part of the city, like a change in the plane of existence. The feeling of going down was frightening, then going back up to the surface into safety. William turned the pills down, and suddenly experienced Kundalini rise (natal Vesta opposition transiting Uranus)!

William's head was tingling (Vesta in Libra/Uranus in Aries). Like a psychic investigator, William was looking for the devil and found it (transiting Ascendant in Pisces and a natal Pluto Yod to transiting Chiron and natal Chiron). A priest got on the bus. William was talking to someone about getting naked at a Beltane festival. A large man violently got in William's face wanting to know where people were getting naked (transiting Jupiter conjunct natal Mars; transiting Mars conjunct natal Chiron). William got off the bus and away from this man. He found himself focusing on a seven-foot-tall man bouncing a tennis ball. William's focus (Vesta) was on the ball. The man bouncing the ball said something odd yet intelligent (Uranus): "It is time to accelerate."

William explained his KR as the Universe telling him, "You must experience this now!" He described his experience as a second version of the "dark night of the soul". Transiting Uranus was in the third temple (community), and natal Uranus was in the 10th house. With transiting Vesta in the 2nd temple William's values changed, he quit the job, and moved on to higher spheres. His natal Vesta is in the ninth temple and he is now a healer.

His third eye and crown chakra activated and felt on fire. William's Kundalini rise was fear-activated, he was losing control without giving up control (Virgo). Transiting North node was conjunct Saturn in the

9th temple. Transiting Chiron was opposition to natal Ceres; healing what is thought of as nurturing.

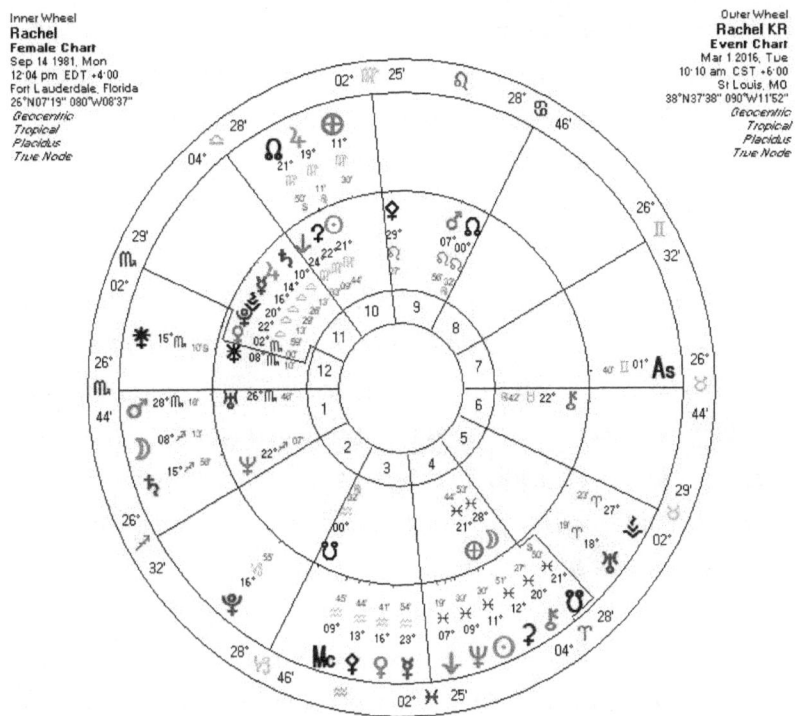

My Kundalini rise was very different. Each person has their own varying experience, and I enjoyed mine, for the most part. It was a healing and powerful turn-on. It was accompanied by much anxiety and inner and outer changes shortly before and after the experience, which lasted days and perhaps months. I believe my kundalini rise was part of my Will. The North node was conjunct my Sun.

Pieces from my Tantra Journal:

I awoke early this morning. I tried going back to sleep, but I was thinking about all the energy over the past weekend. My guru sent me more photos and I can't shake them out of my head. I shared with him my diary—I can't believe I did that!

He said he liked the story of the reflective, glass-top stove. I remember I wrote it right after it happened, making sure to add all the juicy details. All of this makes me so horny.

I put pressure on my clit with my middle finger. My head was spinning. I put my other hand on my belly and caressed it lightly. More pressure, I pulled at and pushed my skin. I wanted to fuck myself.

It started raining outside. I listened to it fall and hit the roof and siding. I imagined it hitting my skin—the pitter-patter of cool drips hitting my body. I went into the other room with a mirror, not being able to take it anymore. I had to love myself, now! I started slowly, watching through the mirror, rubbing my hands across my body. Starting at my jawline, moving down my neck, over my chest, squeezing my nipples between my fingers, pressing harder as I moved down my abdomen. I had to touch her.

I couldn't take it. I began pulling and squeezing my clit with my hand and then between my fingers. I was so wet my middle finger slipped inside without me even trying. It wasn't enough. I watched myself grabbing at my body, "Fuck me," is what I wanted, "Fuck me," I craved it. I pulled my middle finger out, aligned it with my ring finger, and slid them both in, gently at first, letting them soak, and then harder, harder... My mouth opened wide. I wanted to taste myself; the thought of that ruled me. I rubbed my clit with one hand while I fucked myself with the other. I wanted to cum. I was so close. I held it though I wanted it so bad. My mouth was open, and I wanted to suck my fingers; my whole body was vibrating, dancing, shuddering. I felt like I was going to cry. All this hot, sexual energy was driving me wild. I felt like my whole body was sobbing. I didn't actually think I had cried, but I noticed my eyes were wet moments later. I want to do it again, right now!

About 10 minutes after sending this last tidbit in an email to my tantra guru, I went to take a shower. (I have to go get creamy, raw milk, and some more of that awesome, home-made soap from Jersey Jen.) In the bathroom, I removed my clothes and took one glance at myself. It was like I shot one frame in my mind with a film camera and it began to flicker. My body began shuddering again, as if a wave of energy was making it convulse. I touched my body, trying to get a hold on myself. I put my face into my hands. What ... is ... going ... on?!!! I started heating up. I quickly entered the shower thinking it would help, but it just made it more intense. Water was hitting my body, I thought about raindrops, driving me wild. I'm shaking! I felt energy all over me, like someone was there coaxing me. I washed myself clean and couldn't shake this feeling. I turned the water up as hot as it would go. Shivers broke loose all throughout my body, my breath quickened, and I moaned louder than I wanted to. The hot water hitting me was too much. I fell back allowing the energy to flow and the wall to catch me as the steamy water hit my root. So ... much ... energy! I thought I would have another orgasm right then. I am still shivering and shaking. What was that?

Being completely aware intensifies everything. So sensational.

I emailed my guru about it, and my guru told me I had experienced a kundalini rise. I was consumed as I studied it and experienced it. I am forever changed.

3/30/2016: I forgot my dream, something to do with blood and mouth. Yesterday I was putting laundry away. I went into my bathroom/sanctuary to put some towels away. I felt that surge of energy and I just wanted to touch myself. I wanted to feel that kundalini energy again ... I spoke to myself. I don't remember exactly what I said, but it was on the lines of affirmations like "I am powerful" and "I am in control".

Something came to me while studying astrology. Like I am supposed to find all the things I don't like about myself and do something with them ... transmute them, or just maybe accept them.

March 8th, 2017: One year and one week after my kundalini rise. I finally did a natal/transit/progression chart. Transiting Black Moon Lilith conjunct my Natal Vesta, opposed Natal Eris conjunct transiting Uranus (3-1-2016). This is the aspect that resonated the most. I haven't found much information on it except Barbara Hand Clow's book on Kundalini and Astrology. In her book it is the Uranus opposite Uranus transit is when Kundalini energy is most felt. I have over five more years before this occurs. I do not, however, believe that I experienced Kundalini rising before I was ready. It was a pleasant experience for the most part. I am thankful I had a teacher to tell me what had happened to me. I do not know of too many people who have experienced this; just one on a Facebook group. I have asked for dates/times of these happening in others' lives. Nothing thus far.

The Kundalini Rising Charts of Others

March 13th 2017: I have received three charts on others' kundalini rising. Uranus, Lilith, Vesta, and Eris seem the likely luminaries involved during a kundalini rising. All of the charts I read including my own have transiting Uranus opposite their natal Vesta. At the time of my kundalini rise, transiting Lilith was conjunct my natal Vesta. One chart had transiting Lilith conjunct natal Uranus. Matt (very Plutonian), was rather young and had a rough experience. His natal Lilith is conjunct his natal Vesta. In my opinion, he wasn't quite ready, but was already past the point of no return.

Two of the charts have the transiting North Node conjunct Eris in opposition to transiting Jupiter in Libra. Vesta in a natal stellium was also a theme, as well as transiting North Node conjunct natal Eris. Not in my chart, however, the transiting North Node and transiting Jupiter were conjunct my Virgo Sun/Ceres; transiting Uranus was conjunct my natal Eris. Two of the charts have Scorpio rising. One has zero degrees Sagittarius rising, and the other less studied person has 29 degrees Gemini rising (I considered her a Cancer rising). It was difficult trying to get an accurate chart from her; she said it was a transit chart, but it only had one set of planets. Hers and my Vesta stelliums are both in the 11th house. The other two had their Vesta stellium in their 9th house.

What I have found is that this is not something that happens to many people, or perhaps people just do not know or understand what is/has happened. I can see why Barbara Hand Clow would consider the Uranus opposition but so far I have found the common aspect for kundalini rise to be the Uranus/Vesta opposition. However, all of the charts have Vesta stelliums; therefore, Uranus was in aspect/opposite the other planets in the stellium. But Vesta was at the closest degree (exact or near-exact).

I experienced kundalini energy as the outside coming in, for the most part. I believe I cleared a block moments before my kundalini rising. Both Matt and I were practicing a form of activation. I do not know his way of meditation. At the time I did not know Tantra would inspire kundalini rise, and we both had anxiety after the fact. But it seems that we both understand it was an important part of our growth. Also, we both have Scorpio rising.

Pushing kundalini to open before your blocks are clear is potentially dangerous. Matt's experience of kundalini rising was from the inside out, he was feeling as though his insides were coming out, as if the energy he was channeling had too forcefully pushed through his blocks. He was only 28 years old when it occurred. He was bringing it on through a breathing and chakra ritual or practice. He mentioned that his mistake was neglecting his lower chakras.

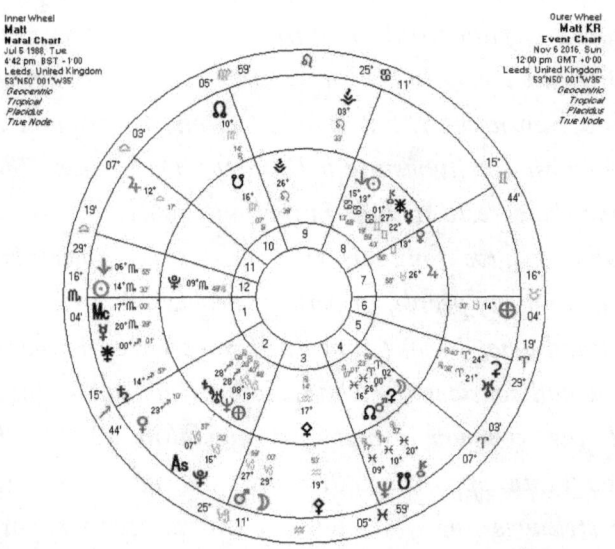

I accidentally pulled a different chart for this person. In the first chart I drew for him, Matt was only 17! But that was when transiting Uranus was opposite his natal Vesta. He was so young, but he still had to experience this. Transiting Uranus at the time of his KR was at 22 degrees, Aries trine his natal Vesta at 26 degrees Leo. Transiting Vesta is conjunct with his Part of Fortune (absent in the chart presented). Transiting Pallas had just passed his natal Pallas (17 degrees Rx) at 20 degrees Aquarius. The transiting North Node is conjunct his natal

Nessus (absent in the chart presented). He knew he had to experience this. He worked to bring it about.

Matt does not have Vesta in a natal stellium. Vesta is nearing the Midheaven in the 9th temple, trine Saturn/Uranus in the 2nd temple, and sextile another stellium. Transiting Vesta was in Leo, and his natal Vesta is also in Leo, sextile Saturn and Uranus. The transiting ascendant conjunct his Natal Neptune. His Natal Pallas is square the transiting MC/Midheaven.

His moon is in the 4th house. Like me, Matt kept a journal. I have saved both, but I have not been able to find Matt, or his journal, on the internet again. Matt shared with me his journal, *Memories of My Kundalini Awaking*. He was practicing breathing and chakra meditation. His root chakra was blocked or closed, and he experienced pain before it opened, "allowing is the key." He felt the sensation of orgasm rising, describing it as "a rising fire." His body temperature elevated as the energy rose to the other chakras.

Senses once obstructed opened up, clear and sound. Matt felt the waves, describing them as musical vibrations changing the molecular structure of water. He may have experienced pain from past trauma again. He describes the Kundalini energy as "intense voltage," perhaps forcefully pushing through his blocks as he summoned it.

I was quick to surrender; his KR took days. Matt describes going inward or focusing within. He also experienced the energy from above; perhaps a connection to Source or Soul Star. Ailments he suffered from before his KR seemed to straighten out or disappear. He mentioned feeling rain droplets falling on him when focusing or relaxing. He tripled his efforts and had an "intense upward pulling" felt in his head/crown. The movement of KR, still present, was intensifying. Matt described many sensations and internal changes. Some of those included the motion of the arm/snake/tongue or KR energy and pains like a nosebleed.

Breath is his way of manifestation. Fear kept holding it back. Daily chores became hard to focus on doing. He also experienced anxiety. He felt his body working internally and described his sensations in great detail; terror, expanding awareness, convulsions, and trembling. He could not control these "aftershocks" either. He had loss of appetite after cravings ceased, and extreme thirst. He could feel his chakras spin, move, enlarge, and shrink.

Matt became more bodily-aware and felt a more intimate connection to his vehicle. "Control continues to improve. Awareness of subtle energies is still increasing. Clearing my mind has become easier while meditating, altered states of consciousness/awareness are almost immediate, sense of acceleration present." He speaks of "Nightmare Consciousness" as the repressed emotional energy rising to the surface for awareness and healing. He experienced heart pain/strain and a kind of personal death. He speaks of the connection of the root and crown chakra and describes a blending of the entire nervous system.

Having a kundalini rising is no easy feat, and everyone I have talked to agrees that it is necessary. It is critical to have some alone time during the psychotic episodes one may experience. Understand that one will never know how strong they are until they have to be.

3/27/2017: I have received another chart. I should have documented it that day. Sara said she wasn't doing anything to bring it on; "it just happened." She said it happened on January 16, but she was not sure if it happened between then and the 19th 2017. Vesta was opposite Eris/Uranus. She has a Vesta stellium in the 2nd house with Sun and Mercury. Sara and Matt both have natal Saturn conjunct natal Uranus. Transiting Saturn (with Pholus) was conjunct Sara's, and sharing the same place in the 4th house with natal Neptune opposes natal Chiron. Saturn return! Natal BML was conjunct the Ascendant, in opposition to transiting Chiron. She's a Pisces Moon like me. Jupiter also plays a large part in Sara's chart. Progressed Venus was conjunct transiting Jupiter and natal Vesta. Her progressed Sun and Vesta are now in Scorpio. Vesta is the fire, Eris the bliss, Uranus the spark, Lilith the drive,

Chiron the healer, Jupiter the opportunity, and Saturn the discipline.

With Vesta retrograde and opposite her Natal Pallas conjunct transiting MC/Midheaven and Sun, Sara said that hers did not go right. It happened prematurely. Both Matt and Sara were experiencing their Saturn return at the time of their KR!

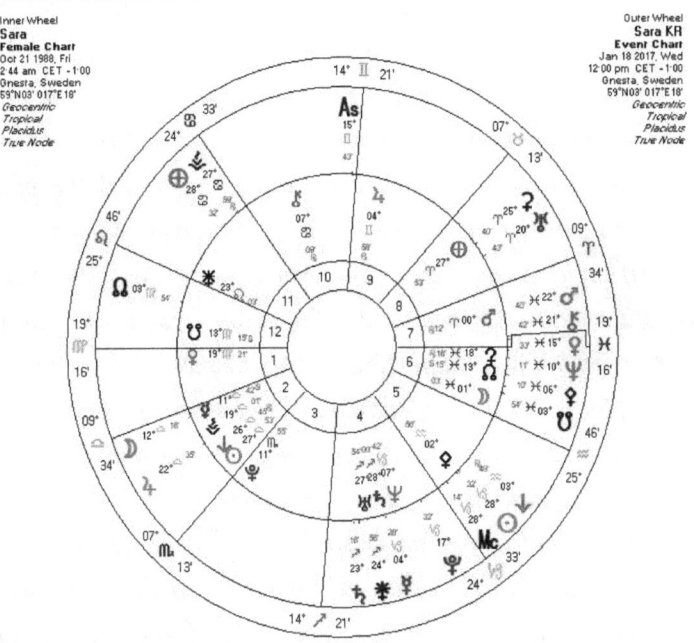

4/7/2017: I cannot sleep. It is after 5 am and I have been awake since 3:30 or earlier. I awoke thinking about my friends and extended family. I love my family and I miss my friends. However, I am at the point in my life (mid 30s-early 40s) where I need and relish my time alone; in my work, meditation, being present in beautiful surroundings. I often seek opportunities to go for rides by myself. I used to not like being alone, sole errand runner, but now I look forward to it. I am thankful for astrology. It has helped me to learn about important life passages, and how to navigate through them. I know, at this

particular time in my life, it is a time to learn about myself and know myself. Social awkwardness isn't so bad now that I know it is okay to be alone.

I used to feel lonely when I had no one else around, but I am not lonesome anymore even when I am alone. I am more aware of Universal law and the energy that flows through me. Nature is my best teacher for nothing stands still in complete awareness. By connecting with myself and the Earth, I am aware of small vibrations. I pay attention to them. Even minute, they are most important. When touching the ground, I feel many sensations. Tasting a wild edible, I feel the plant's vibrations and its effect on me. I have become more aware of how different people affect me. Sometimes I feel the need to escape a certain presence, or daydream as I watch the sunset or other gorgeous natural setting. I like to meditate on the river flowing; it is constantly changing. I like hearing the sound it makes as it passes over rocks and drops with a splash, releasing negative ions and creating a positive mood.

Later: I had to remind myself to be present. It took a little time and I tried to get as comfortable as I could. I dangled my upper body and left arm over the edge of the chair while I massaged my clit with my right hand. I relaxed as completely as I was able. I moaned loudly as full awareness opened me up ... I felt his kundalini as I concentrated on my injection. My root chakra was open as my energy shot to my sacral, power in my solar plexus, love/green/heart, back to solar plexus yellow, green heart, lapis/throat "uh!", my eyes are open, violet/third eye, crown ... The violent shaking came over me. My whole body vibrated with erotic energy. My body moved against his as I controlled the rhythm and the beat. I could feel his rising as he began to move to his rhythm. My head turned back and forth almost violently as the energy shot through me, all the way up, and out of my crown Chakra. My voice flowed freely as my orgasm released.

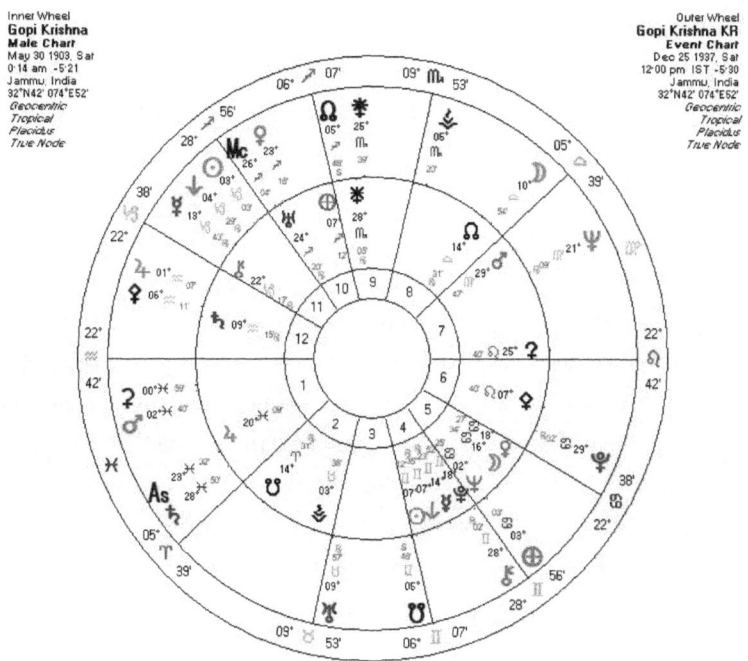

The Uranus opposition occurs once in a lifetime, at about age 40-42. It takes 84 years for Uranus to orbit the Sun. If my theory is correct, the average person will have only one chance (three if retrograde) to experience the transiting Uranus opposition to natal Vesta. Kundalini risings are common, but they do not occur for everyone. Some may argue that they do. I have met a couple of other people born the same year (and near the same time) who have also experienced Kundalini rising while writing this book. Although an important transit, I cannot be sure that everyone experiences kundalini rise at their Uranus opposition (about age 40, a.k.a. the midlife crisis). Note the transiting nodal placements in the charts, not just the stelliums; many have Pisces transiting stelliums. Transiting Vesta is often very prominent.

The author of *Kundalini: The Evolutionary Energy in Man*, Gopi Krishna, does not have Vesta in a stellium, but transiting Vesta was in opposition to transiting Uranus when he reported Kundalini rising. Transiting Uranus was conjunct the natal Vesta. His rising was a little different (they all are). He asked many gurus and holy men about his experience, and they denied that he had a kundalini rise. To each their own! It is my opinion that he did indeed. His book is a reference to understanding your own KR. After the change, you have new knowledge to comprehend, and the experienced can direct their will and this powerful, energetic force.

The Hugging Guru, Mātā Amṛtānandamayī Devī (born Sudhamani Idamannel), Amma, or Ammaji, may have experienced a Kundalini rise early in life. People come to her, and she accepts them and offers a shoulder to cry on and hugs to all. Scolded by her parents for giving their belongings away to the poor, Amma desired to give anything she could to help others suffering. Her family could not afford to keep her and sent her away. She was five, almost six years old at the time transit Uranus opposed her natal Vesta.

Transiting Uranus opposed her natal Vesta at 16 degrees Leo. Her natal Vesta is at 16 degrees 27 minutes Aquarius. Transiting Vesta traveled over Uranus in 1959 before transiting Uranus opposed her natal Vesta (*see chart*). Ceres is conjunct Jupiter on her Ascendant and square transit Uranus and natal Vesta; Neptune is conjunct the Ascendant, and she has a Yod to Vesta natally (BML sextile Uranus). She has a powerful stellium in her 10th house (Ceres/Venus/Mars).

As of April of 2019, Amma ("mother"), the hugging guru, has hugged more than 37 million people worldwide. From lepers to the wealthy and famous, she embraces all who come to her. She is also known to give chocolate kisses (my favorite) and rose petals. Ammachi has done much to lift the poor by opening healing centers and schools in India. "...By affecting individuals, you can make changes in the society and, through it, in the world," Amṛtānandamayī herself says.

Action, knowledge, and devotion are her sacred essentials. Through her teachings, typically of the Vedas, she accepts all various spiritual teachings. All paths lead to a common goal: transcendence and a purifying of the mind/body. Her focused meditation is through songs; she has Scorpio and Neptune rising and a Taurus moon. Meditation, service, and the divine are sacred to her. She practices compassion, self-control, forgiveness, and kindness. By refining the mind, we come to the understanding of consciousness. We are not our mind/body. We are eternal energy of "non-dual substratum". She believes we reach this state by living. Jivanmukti, or universal bliss of conscious enlightenment, achieved while living in the body, allows one to merge with the infinite upon death. We leave the wheel of life and death. Many believe that some of these enlightened individuals decide to come back to help others reach this state.

Amṛtānandamayī has done a lot of "Vestal" work in her years. She understands the state of the world and the importance of environmental protection, ecology, and community. She is involved in spiritual and worldly issues, such as desegregating science and spirituality, gender equality, and the idea of being a mother to all living beings. Her followers believe her to be a saint.

I have come to realize that a humble life is spiritual, and that taking care of the people and the home is most important. I am strengthened by taking charge of what I want and challenging what I need. Self-controlled, surrender, and serenity showed me my path, either selfless giving or a lone traveler. Each person experiences KR by releasing blocks. Whatever it is that they have repressed. Emotions, sexuality, pain, ect.; these things will release and give way to the flow of energy.

The Dissolution of Ego

Dissolution of the ego is bringing ourselves under our control. It begins with detaching. It is the beginning of true renunciation, and it occurs when one pulls themselves back into themselves. What happens over time, when boundaries are not determined, we become attached to people or things, often to the point that we may lose some of ourselves in them if we are not careful.

Part of the dissolution would include Vesta/Durga. From within, we call on her, Oh Powerful Devi. She is the destroyer of demons and limitations. She is in her most beautiful, powerful state, the virgin controlling her lion. She has strength and poise and is ready to take on the illusions in the world. She is confident and calm and draws on her feminine power from within herself. Each aspect of her personality overcomes each demon that tempts her. She will succeed, Oh Shiny One! The gods have no other choice. She does her work.

Dissolution of the false Ego is sensing what we perceive as real, but we do not need the false ego. Everyone has an ego, and it is good to have an ego. We are coming to terms with those egoistic desires; the car, money, job, reputation, social situation, persona, emotions, such as fear, guilt, shame, etc. These are the things on the outside. When we are centered and purified, the false ego has no power over us. We have separated ourselves from what lies outside of the temple.

Losing the things you love is a spiritual experience because the lost were of the material world, husband, career, false ego. I know I have to keep living until I can escape the wheel. I must face my demons.

Losing the things I loved turned into me hating the evil in the world. I wanted to take on the injustice and kill it; feeling Kali, I quested to seek and destroy demons. I believe I am feeling not just my, but the earth's yearning as well. Something has to be deconstructed first before something new is structured. Vesta's giving up her seat (ego) to attend (devotion) to the flame (sacred feminine) of the earth is a representation of ego dissolution.

Vesta has a way of not holding on to anything. She has to give up her pride/ego to advance spiritually. Take off the mask and tend to the sacred. Hestia gave up her position in heaven to another god (Dionysus). She seemed satisfied enough to attend to the sacred fire with devotion. Many with Vesta prominent in their chart may experience some dissolution often in their lives, and renunciation may also be a theme.

We may hold onto things until we want to let them go. If we do not want to let them go, then there is still attachment. Attachment is a human thing to have, but we do not wish to become unattached to ourselves. "Wherever you go, there you are." People, places, and things come and go, but you must go on or stay "stuck" and unmoving. When one is not creating or sustaining, it is the destruction that ensues.

The dissolution of the ego is part of our healing process to remove blocks and veils. The light shines brighter in the dark through suffering or conscious transformation. We experience pain to be able to dissolve the false ego and gain empathy. This is the fall from the great heights of the tower; when our pride is humbled, we can shine our brightest. Our soul shines through when our ego steps out of the way. Even our dark side is present. We are allowed to see who we truly are, and we can decide to change if we so choose.

Epilogue: The Will of Vesta

"Love is the guide of thy will", and a Vestal must learn how to invest in her will. She must know her plan and then devote herself to its realization, not unlike the Magician. Practice meditation while at work; review the work. Bring the unconscious to the conscious and the conscious to the unconscious. Use wisdom in all thy works, especially logic with intuition when considering the unknown.

There is always a constant back and forth to unity and independence. To learn the will of Vesta, or where one's focus lies, one must experience both. To know who she is, her sexuality, her ego, and then to understand who others are, their sexuality, and their ego (or vice versa) is to find the divine will. When you are clear with yourself on who you are and who others are, you will recognize your connection with them and understand the divine meaning or message.

There is a romance in giving oneself to God/Goddess. A Vestal is loyal to the one. If a Vestal is married to herself, the Goddess/God, or the church or Pontifex Maximus, she is in love and devoted. Acceptance is the key. Nothing happens *to* you, but things happen *because of* you. Accept yourself, as well as others; we are how we are now. Honor your free will and the free will of all! Visualize where you want to be; look forward to happiness, and create what you love.

I wonder if it is the essence of Vesta herself that I am feeling or my past that I am healing. I know it is how it is at this moment. I cannot deny the feeling of sensual, utter devotion! I am hers as she gives herself to me in all her might! To be Shakti and be with Shiva is to unite in an ever-flowing organic state of mind! It is the divine union of consciousness. That is my Will! Blessings on the pursuit of yours!

References

- Clow, B. (2013). Astrology and the Rising of Kundalini: The transformative power of Saturn, Chiron, and Uranus. Rochester: Bear & Company.
- Donath, E. B. (1979). Asteroids in the Birth Chart. Tempe: American Federation of Astrologers, Inc.
- Donath, E. B. (1977). Asteroids in Synastry. Dayton: Geminian Institute.
- George, D. (1986). Asteroid Goddesses. San Diego: ACS Publications, Inc.
- Krishna, G. (1985). Kundalini: The evolutionary energy in man. Boston: Shambhala.
- Mookerjee, A. (1988). Kali: The feminine force. Rochester:Destiny Books. Reed, C.L. (2004).
- Unveiled: The hidden lives of nuns. New York: Berkley Books.
- Oken, A. (1976). Astrology: evolution and revolution a path to higher consciousness through astrology. Toronto: Bantam Books.
- Rathus, S. A., Nevid, J. S., Rathus, L. F. (2002). Human sexuality: In a world of diversity (5th ed.). Boston: Pearson
- Rock, William Pennell. "Jealousy and the Abyss." Journal of Humanistic Psychology Vol. 23, No. 2 (1983): 70-84. Reprinted by www.planetwaves.net, Association for Humanistic Psychology.
- Stone, M. (1976). When God Was a Woman. Barnes and Noble.
- Wildfang, R. L. (2006). Rome's Vestal Virgins: A study of Rome's Vestal priestesses in the late republic and early empire. New York: Rouledge.
- Wescott, M.L. (1988). Mechanics of the Future: Asteroids. Massachusetts: Treehouse Mountain.
- Wescott, M.L. (1993). The Orders of Light. Massachusetts: Treehouse Mountain.
- https://planetwaves.net/news/daily-astrology/vesta-astrology/
- https://theinnerwheel.com/2011/05/20/driven-towards-the-sacred-vesta-part-two/
- https://www.visionpubl.com/en/cities/temple-of-vesta/